Portuguese Style of Knitting

History, Traditions and Techniques

Published in 2010 by
Andrea Wong Knits, Powell, Ohio

© 2010 by Andrea Wong
All rights reserved.

No part of this publication may be reproduced, stored in a retrieval system, or transmitted in any form or by any means, electronic, mechanical, photocopying, recording, or otherwise, without prior written permission of the copyright holder.

ISBN: 978-0-615-36489-6

Concept, writing and production: Andrea Wong
Technical pattern editing: Therese Chynoweth
Proofreading: Katie Banks
Diagrams: Therese Chynoweth
Charts: Therese Chynoweth, Andrea Wong, Katherine Misegades.
Photography:
 In Portugal: Andrea Wong
 Of techniques: Paul Wong
 Other images: Tita Costa, Katherine Misegades, Tracy Holroyd-Smith, and Museu Nacional de Arqueologia; Instituto dos Museus e da Conservação, I.P. / Ministério da Cultura;
 Fotógrafo: José Pessoa
Graphic design/print production: Katherine Misegades

Printed in Canada

Portuguese Style of Knitting

History, Traditions and Techniques

By
Andrea Wong

Andrea Wong Knits
Powell, Ohio

I dedicate this book to
my husband, Paul, and my children, Alex and Ana,
for their constant support and understanding.

Acknowledgments

I would like to thank all of the people who contributed to the publication of this book in one way or another:

❈ First to my mother who introduced me to knitting, thank you for teaching me the craft that became my passion and my business.

❈ My thanks also goes to all of my students who taught me so much in the process.

❈ Also thank you dear friends who watched me, coached me, helped me and prayed for me even before I started writing this book.

❈ To Karen Wilkins who was the first to believe in me and my talent, I extend a special thanks.

❈ A huge thank you to Tita Costa and the knitters from Porto, Portugal.

❈ My deep appreciation goes to my layout artist and editor, Katherine Misegades, to my pattern editor, Therese Chynoweth, and to all of the visionary authors who inspired me.

❈ And last but not least to my saint Teresa de Avila, who I know has helped in many ways so I could work and write, thank you.

Andrea Wong

Table of Contents

6	Foreword
7	Introduction
8	Portuguese History and Culture
13	The Portuguese Style of Knitting
13	A Brief History of Knitting and the Portuguese Style
14	The Knitting Needles: Hooked or Not
14	The Knitting Pin
16	The Basic Technique
16	How to Set Up
17	Portuguese Cast On
18	The Purl Stitch
19	Purl Through the Back Loop
20	The Knit Stitch
21	Knit Through the Back Loop
22	Ribbing
24	Increases
33	Decreases
36	Portuguese Bind Off
37	Advanced Techniques
37	Knitting with Two Colors
38	Working two-color knitting with knit side facing
38	How to trap main color
40	How to trap background color
42	Working two-color knitting with purl side facing
42	How to trap main color
44	How to trap background color
46	Cables
48	Double Knitting
51	The Advantages of Working With Hooked Needles
50	Binding off as crochet
51	Knitting from right to left needle
52	Portuguese Spinning
54	Portuguese-Inspired Patterns
56	Design Inspiration
57	Abbreviations and Chart Key
58	Cloud Mittens and Scarf
62	Juliana's Baby Sweater
66	Manuela Scarf
69	Traditional Fisherman Sweater
76	Rooster Mittens
80	Traditional Socks
80	Rustic Socks
82	Lacy Socks
84	Sidewalk Mosaic Headband
86	Cascais Woman's Vest
90	Bibliography
91	Yarn and Needle Sources
92	Index

Foreword

by Katherine Misegades

Andrea's book offers us several gifts. First, it takes us on a tour of Portugal with photos and a brief history. Next, it introduces us to techniques not commonly seen in most of the Americas. Third, it offers us a ready reference and patterns that we can use to practice techniques that might be new to us.

I love knitting books that offer more than just knitting patterns. I love book tours to other countries and cultures. I love to study how other people developed techniques and how they do their work.

One of my artisan friends was a Cherokee master woodcarver. I sat next to him, pocket knife and a piece of walnut in hand, and learned more than how to whittle a little bird with a graceful neck. I learned how he continuously expanded his skills and knowledge. Even though he was in his eighties at the time, was considered at the top of his field, and had taught many students over the years, he'd kept learning from *everyone, everywhere*. He traveled the world visiting woodcarvers. He adopted a technique here and a new way to use a tool there. He practiced and polished his craft as he incorporated the best from each encounter.

So it is with knitting. We can learn, grow, polish our techniques, and adopt new ways and designs. We can enjoy the endless variations on the simplest theme of knitting—knit and purl stitches.

Page 6 photos:
Left—The Oriente Train Station in Lisbon was completed in 1998 and is one of the world's largest stations.
Right—The triumphal arch in Praça do Comércio leads into Rua Augusta e A Baixa.

Page 7 photos:
Left—Modernized antique streetcars run very well on electricity through the narrow streets of Lisbon.
Right—This tile panel is on a street wall in downtown Lisbon.

Introduction

It was my mother, Maria Jose R. Amadeo, who taught me how to knit when I was seven years old. I grew up in a two-bedroom apartment in Sao Paulo, Brazil and, not having a backyard or room to play, she had other ways to keep me entertained. I remember my first piece of knitting—a yellow triangle of garter stitch lace. It was not supposed to be triangular nor was it supposed to be lacy. I learned the purl stitch first because it was the easiest when using the technique my mother taught me. For me, garter stitch is purling every row.

Knitting was then part of my life wherever I went. I married Paul in 1988. A year after the wedding he was transferred to the south of Brazil. We knew we were going to spend a year there before moving to the United States, so I did not look for a job. I did what I always wanted to do: learn how to swim correctly and improve my knitting. My teacher was the first one to point out to me that only people from Sao Paulo knit the way I knit. In the south of Brazil, due to the strong influence of German immigrants, they knit Continental style.

When I came to the United States in 1991, I was approached by many knitters who were curious about the way I knit. Besides the English (or American) and Continental (or German) styles, there are others, which include this less known way. The Portuguese differs from the other styles because it relies on holding the yarn around the neck or around a hook pinned on the left shoulder, and wrapping the working yarn using the left thumb.

I started teaching this technique about seven years ago, and have produced three DVDs on the subject. In response to requests from many students, I have written this reference book that can be carried in a knitting bag. I actually hope to give you more than the knitting technique—I hope to introduce you to the Portuguese culture as well. I hope you enjoy it!

Portuguese History & Culture

Traveling around modern Portugal, one can see the influence of the various groups of people who have contributed to Portugal's history. The Celts influenced folklore in the northern region, and the Moors influenced Fado music. Vestiges of Celtic language remain in the modern language. Olive trees, tiles and cooking methods were brought by the Moors. Chestnut trees and grape vines were introduced by the Romans. Portugal's romantic language, beautiful architecture (including its dazzling azulejos and calçadas), paintings and distinguished literature also testify to a wide variety of these influences.

Portugal's rich culture dates back to prehistoric times. Men appeared in what is now Portugal during the Old Stone Age. Thousands of years later the Celts came, and brought a small group of Germans with them settling mostly in the north of the Iberian Peninsula known as Galicia. Some of the round stone houses they lived in can still be seen there.

These Celts, who came to be known as Lusitanians, had a similar culture to the groups already in Iberia. At about the same time, in the southern region of Portugal, the Phoenicians founded settlements, and were followed by the Greeks and Carthaginians. The Greeks called the peninsula Iberia which included Portugal and Spain but the Romans eventually took the region and named it Hispania (or Lusitania). The Romans brought Latin with them—the roots of the Portuguese language—as well as the road networks that formed the basis of today's motorways and connections to the rest of Europe. The Moors, who came from north Africa, were inspired by Mohammed who

Left—The Portuguese flag has two vertical bands of green and red with the Portuguese coat of arms centered on the dividing line.
Right—This knot pattern adorns one of the internal patio windows on the Cathedral da Sé.

had died only 79 years earlier. By 700, their forces had swept across North Africa and subdued Morocco. They crossed into what is now modern Spain in 711, and rapidly subjugated almost the entire peninsula. The Moors held power in Portugal and Spain for the next four centuries. To this day, their strong influence can be seen in the Alentejo and Algarve provinces.

Over the years, the Christians reconquered several areas from the north to the southern end of the peninsula. Several Christian kingdoms were formed. In the eleventh century, Alfonso VI, the ruler of the kingdom of Leon and Castile, established the County of Portucale (the origin of the word for *Portugal*) between the rivers Douro and Mondego. Later Portucale was declared a separate kingdom.

In the thirteenth century, the Portuguese finally completed the reconquest of Portugal. Many of the Moors continued to live in Portugal and converted to Christianity. In 1492, the Portuguese expelled the Moors.

Colonial expansion began in Africa under King João. These expeditions and discoveries made Portugal the leading maritime and colonial power in western Europe. Lisbon developed into a major commercial city. Prince Henry the Navigator also promoted voyages of discovery, and founded his school of navigation in Sagres.

With the invention of the caravel, a type of ship, the Portuguese were the first Europeans to open the way into the Atlantic. They discovered the islands of Madeira, the Azores, and Cape Verde. Then they sailed to western Africa and crossed the equator. Bartolomeu Dias rounded and named the Cape of Good Hope. Vasco da Gama reached India by sea from the west. Pedro Alvares Cabral discovered Brazil in 1500.

The Portuguese were the first Westerners in Ceylon, Sumatra, Malacca, Timor and the islands of the Moluccas. They were the first Europeans to trade with China and Japan. They established a trading post in Macao which was the first European settlement in China and part of Portugal until 1999.

The Portuguese reached Newfoundland in 1500.

Left–This view is from the patio of the University of Coimbra in Lisbon. It is one of the oldest universities in Europe and the world.
Right–Cascais Bay attracts tourists to enjoy the sea.

Sailing for Spain, the Portuguese explorer Magalhães was the first to circumnavigate the globe. Cabrilho was the first to explore the coast of California.

Thanks to worldwide trade, Portugal enjoyed prosperity, making it the wealthiest country in Europe. It was during this period that Manuel I introduced the Manueline style in the architecture that we see in the Mosteiro dos Jeronimos.

In 1568 at age fourteen, Sebastian was crowned King of Portugal. By the late 1570s, the now wild and fanatical King Sebastian led a disastrous attempt to dominate Morocco. The invasion led to his death and the destruction of all but one hundred of his army of over 20,000. His successor on the throne, Cardinal Henrique, died and the royal succession went to the Spanish Habsburgs. All of the Iberian Peninsula was brought under Spanish rule with the ascension of Philip II of Spain. Philip promised the separation of the two governments and lived up to his promise, but under his son and grandson, Spain let the English and the Dutch take Portugal's valuable foreign possessions. This marks the end of Portugal's golden age.

It was only in 1668 that the Treaty of Lisbon acknowledged Portuguese independence.

In 1755 a devastating earthquake destroyed Lisbon. The prime minister at the time, Marques of Pombal, organized the rebuilding of the city. By the next century, the country was going through better times.

When Napoleon declared an obstruction of English trade, the English responded with a continental blockade. Napoleon insisted that the Portuguese close their ports to the English, opening them only to the Spanish and the French ships, or he would invade Portugal. Because Portugal had always had a good relationship with England, she procrastinated. Napoleon invaded Portugal through Spain. France and Spain agreed that, after the invasion, Portugal would be divided between the two of them. The French occupied the country in 1807, and the Portuguese royal family and court fled to Brazil where the Portuguese monarch, Dom João I, transferred his government. Dom João I was the only European monarch to rule

Left—These are the elegant double arches in the Gothic cloister at the Sé Cathedral.
Right—This tile work on a building on Largo Rafael Bordalo Pinheiro features figures of science, agriculture, industry and commerce.

from the Americas. The colony of Brazil was elevated to the status of a ruling power under the title of the United Kingdom of Portugal, Brazil and Algarve. In 1808 Portugal got help from the British, her oldest ally. Defensive lines were built around Lisbon. When Napoleon reached the fortifications, he retreated. With the aid of the British, Dom João I was the only European monarch of a country invaded by Napoleon not to be deposed. After the war a new constitution was proclaimed, and Dom João I, the royal family, and the court returned to Portugal. Dom João I left his son, Dom Pedro I, to rule Brazil as regent king and Brazil was given independence on September 7th, 1822.

During the years that followed, Portugal suffered political confusion. The beginning of the twentieth century was marked by a radical, nationalist republican movement. In 1908, the king and crown prince were assassinated. In 1910, after an uprising by military officers, Portugal was declared a republic. During World War I Portugal joined the Allies, and in the postwar years, political chaos deepened. Between 1910 and 1945 there were 45 changes of government, and military intervention. In 1932 Antonio Salazar became prime minister, and during World War II, Portugal was declared neutral. Salazar ruled the country for 36 years, banning political parties, establishing censorship and keeping society in order. Opposition was suppressed. In 1968, Salazar suffered a stroke and Marcelo Caetano came to power. Several hundred military officers rebelled on April 25, 1974. There were many governments after that, and the country was only stabilized in the mid-1980s.

In 1986 Portugal joined the European Economic Community. With European Union funds, Portugal became the European Union's fastest growing country.

Left–This is the Monument to the Discoveries on Belem Waterfront. It was dedicated in 1960 during the 500th-year memorial of the death of Prince Henry the Navigator. The monument commemorates the explorers who participated in voyages of discovery. It is a part of a larger complex of pavement and statuary displays. Right–This arched building is on the edge of Alfama, the stalls of the so-called Thieves Market or Feira da Ladra.

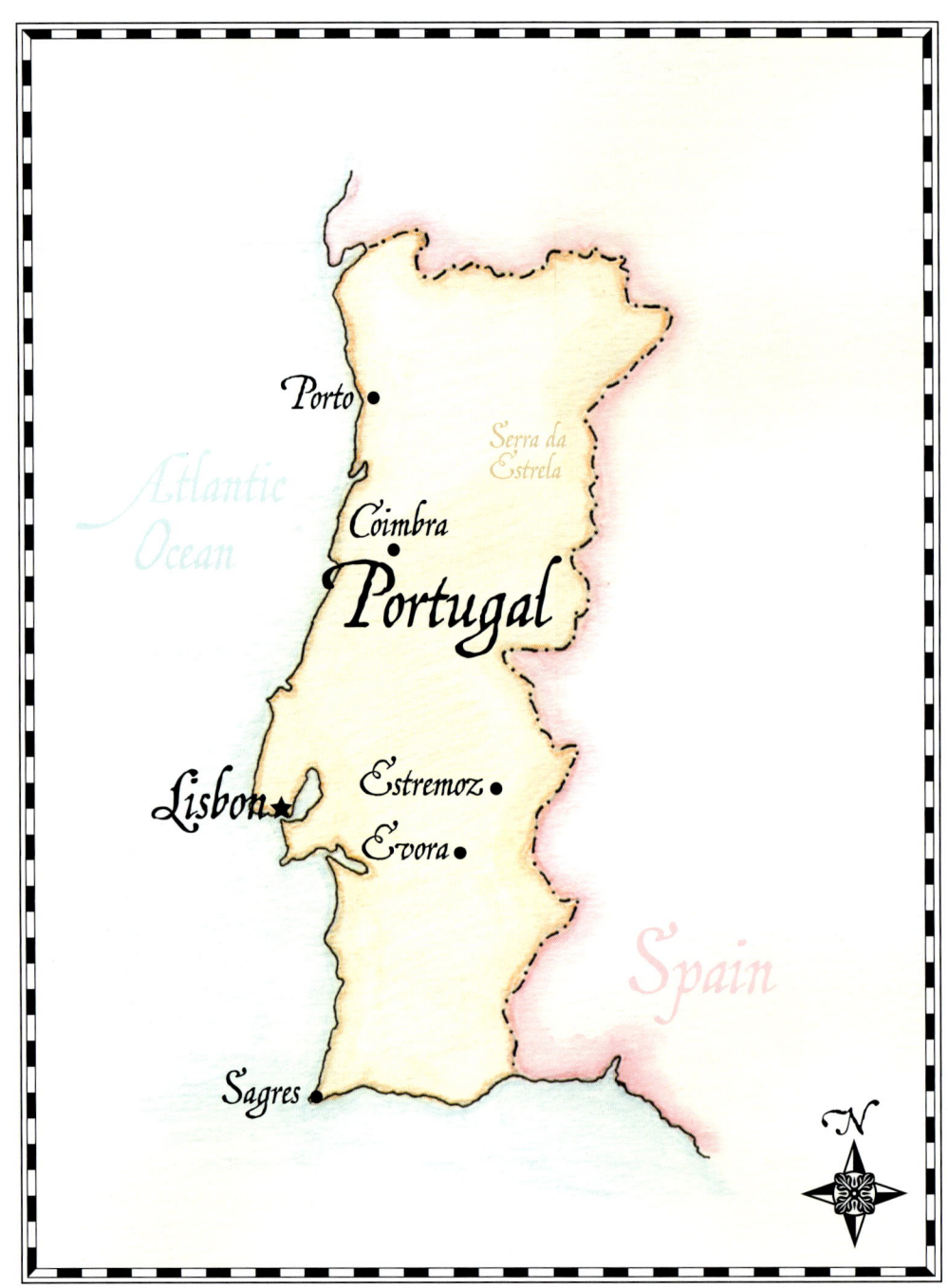

The Portuguese Style of Knitting

Since there are significant variations in techniques within and between countries, a geographic denomination is not an ideal way to name a knitting style, but I decided to do so because my mother learned to knit this style from a Portuguese lady, D. Emma.

Knitting with the yarn around the neck or around a hooked pin is the predominant style of knitting in Portugal, but not the only one. It is a style rarely seen in the Americas but, according to Montse Stanley, this way of holding the work is also popular in areas of Greece, rural Egypt and among the Peruvian Indians of Taquile Island. Mary Thomas writes that it can also be seen among shepherds in the south of France. I have met people from Bulgaria who knit this way as well.

In my quest to know more about the Portuguese style of knitting, I could find no resources containing specific references to this technique except for two books that explain the "Peruvian" or "Portuguese" purl.

A Brief History of Knitting and the Portuguese Style

Knitting is a simple craft and does not require much—simply yarn and two or more needles. It is a relatively new craft when compared with spinning and weaving. Many samples of early fabrics appear to be knitted but turn out to be cross-knit looping. The earliest examples of true knitting date from the second half of the thirteenth century.

All the references I read indicate that knitting started somewhere in the Middle East and then spread into Europe, and finally arrived in the Americas only five hundred years ago with Portuguese and Spanish colonization which started in 1500 AD. The craft of knitting is believed to have originated in Islamic cultures. Anna Zilboorg explains in her book, *Fancy Feet: Traditional Knitting Patterns of Turkey*, "...the spread of knitting mirrored the spread of Islam."

There are two theories about how knitting arrived in Portugal. One suggests that Arabs taught the

Portuguese Style of Knitting

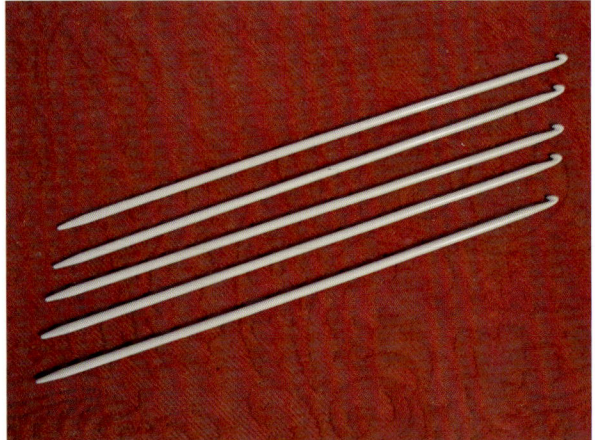

This is a set of five double pointed needles that are still used in Portugal.

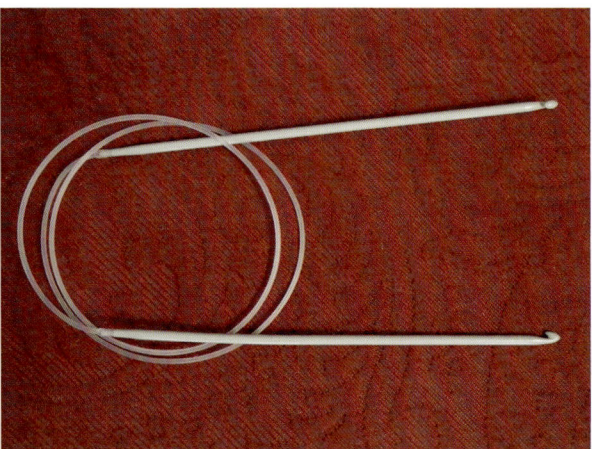

These are circular needles with hooks.

Coptic Christians a craft that is similar to knitting (whether it was real knitting has been contested), and they in turn took this knowledge with them to Europe. Traders also carried the craft from Egypt to Spain and Portugal. From there knitting spread to Italy, England, France, other parts of Europe, and the Americas. Another theory is that the invasion of the Moors brought the craft to Portugal and, during four centuries of Moorish control, the native Portuguese adopted Moorish knitting techniques.

Knitting Needles: Hooked or Not

Early knitting was done with hooked needles made of copper wire with hooks at one end like a crochet hook. Hooked needles are still used to this day in Egyptian villages, Turkey, Bulgaria, places around the Cusco area of Peru, and in rural Portugal. These needles originated in the Middle East, and made working the purl stitch very easy. That is why in some countries like Peru, stranded color knitting designs are worked with the purl side facing the knitter with the yarn tensioned around the neck. The knitter purls every round. The Peruvians make their needles out of bicycle spokes, and the French sometimes use old umbrella ribs.

The Knitting Pin (Alfinete)

In some countries like Brazil and Portugal, knitters thread the yarn around a knitting pin instead of around the neck to keep the yarn from rubbing directly against the skin, and to maintain even tension.

Richard Rutt, in his book, *A History of Hand Knitting*, mentions a Swiss male knitter named Dubois who worked with hooked needles in a very fast manner. The text says: "He kept his ball of yarn in one pocket, held the yarn in light tension under his arm, passing it through a horn ring hooked on his left breast."

Mary Thomas's Knitting Book states, regarding illustrations of a knitting shepherd, "The ancient weather beaten knitting pouch is also from Landes, and is the same as that still used by all the shepherds in this

Hooked Needles, The Knitting Pin

district.... The knitting is kept in this pouch, which is worn slung round the neck with a long leather strap, to which is affixed a hook in the front. In knitting, the yarn is passed over this hook and then round the left thumb, and in and out the fingers on the left hand, for these shepherds operate the wool with the left thumb, in what we might assume was the orthodox method used when hook needles were in vogue."

I found little about the origin of the knitting pin, but I did find pictures of old versions of it. The antique pins did not have a hook like the ones we use today. Instead, they had a hole for the yarn. When a knitter started a new project, she threaded the yarn through the hole in the pin, and then attached the pin to her garment using a ribbon or a crocheted chain. The knitting pin was attached to the project until the yarn was cut.

As years passed, I started collecting knitting pins. They have similar shapes, and can be made of wire or stainless steel. Some manufacturers add beads or embellishments. When I knit using two colors, I thread each color on a different pin—one on my left shoulder and one on my right shoulder.

This knitter tensions her yarn around her neck instead of over a shoulder pin.

Knitting pins

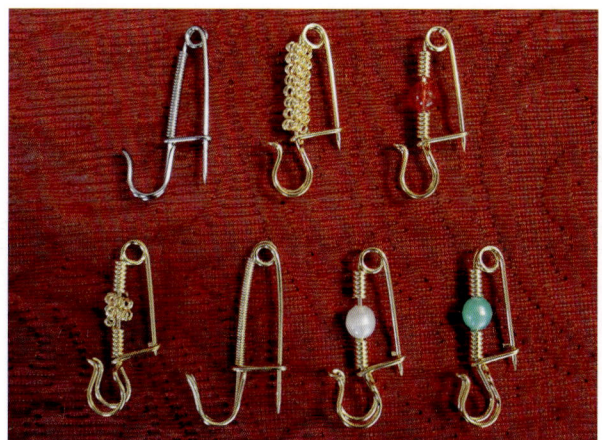

These knitting pins from the 19th and 20th centuries are made of bone and have several holes through which to pass the yarn. Museu Nacional de Arqueologia; Instituto dos Museus e da Conservação, I.P. / Ministério da Cultura; Fotógrafo: José Pessoa

The Basic Technique

The Portuguese style of knitting offers significant advantages:

- Purling is easier than knitting. Many knitters avoid projects that include purling, especially if they knit Continental style.
- It is ergonomic. Keep in mind that knitting is a two handed activity so it does not matter if you are right- or left-handed. With the Portuguese style, you use your left thumb the most, and move your hands less.
- In addition to making your tension even, the neck-tensioning technique makes it easy to work with multiple colors.
- It is easier for the vision impaired knitter since the yarn is always available at the tip of her finger.

Even though Portuguese knitters still use hooked needles, I don't use them regularly. I found that there are some advantages in using them only after meeting with the knitters in Portugal. You can practice this style of knitting using your favorite pair of needles—circular or straight—and any material.

How to Set Up

Before you start, let's make sure you are set up correctly to work. Here are some hints for you to make sure your knitting is going to flow smoothly:

- Knit or purl stitches from the left needle onto the right needle just like you would do with other styles of knitting.
- Place the knitting pin on your left shoulder close to your collar bone. The open part of the hook has to be facing up like a fishing hook.
- Take the working yarn from the work, pass the yarn around your neck *or* knitting pin from left to right, then lay the yarn around your middle finger on your right hand. That's one way to improve tension, which is the essential to this way of knitting. You can also increase or decrease tension by moving the work farther from or closer to you *and/or* controlling how you let the yarn flow through your right hand.

Notice that my knitting pin is attached to my left shoulder when I use one color. Also, my yarn is threaded from my work, around the knitting pin on my shoulder, and around my right middle finger.

Portuguese Cast On

Casting on is the first step in knitting, but the Portuguese cast on may be easier to master after learning the purl stitch. You are welcome to use the cast on you prefer to start your practice, and then come back later and learn the Portuguese cast on.

The Portuguese cast on is like the long-tail cast on except that purl bumps face you as you cast on. If you consider the cast on as your first row, then your purl bumps will be on the public side of the work. Many knitters who use the long-tail cast on work one row to get the most pleasant looking side facing the public.

Hint: To calculate the length of tail to start with, wrap the yarn around the needle 10 times in a spiral. Measure the length of yarn used in this operation. Multiply this length by the number of stitches to be cast on, then divide by 10.

1 Make a loop of yarn around your left index finger leaving the tail hanging below your left hand. Place your working yarn around your neck (or pin) from left to right.

2 Insert your right hand needle into the loop from right to left. Wrap the working yarn counterclockwise around the right needle using your left thumb.

3 Bring the yarn through the loop and toward the back to complete the stitch. Repeat this process until you have the desired number of stitches on your right hand needle.

Portuguese Style of Knitting

The Purl Stitch

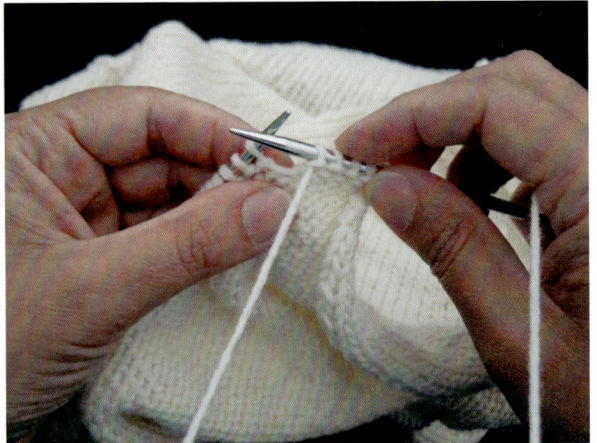

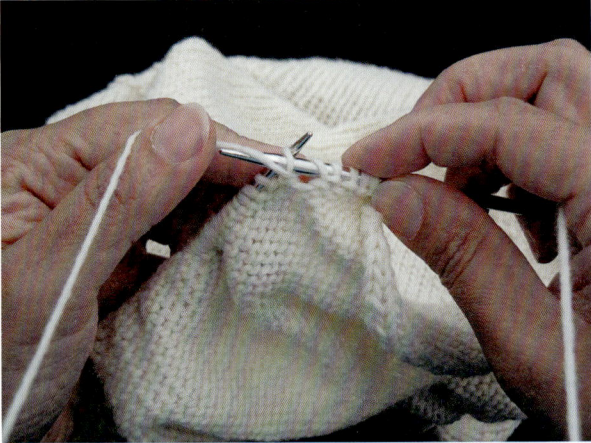

1 Insert the right hand needle into the front of the loop of the first stitch on the left hand needle (the same way you insert it for the English or Continental style of knitting).

2 Using your left thumb, flick the yarn around the top of the right hand needle counterclockwise.

Most of my students agree that this way of purling is easier and faster than the English or Continental styles. Some students like the knit stitch even better!

Important note: The working yarn should be below (or in front of) the right hand needle.

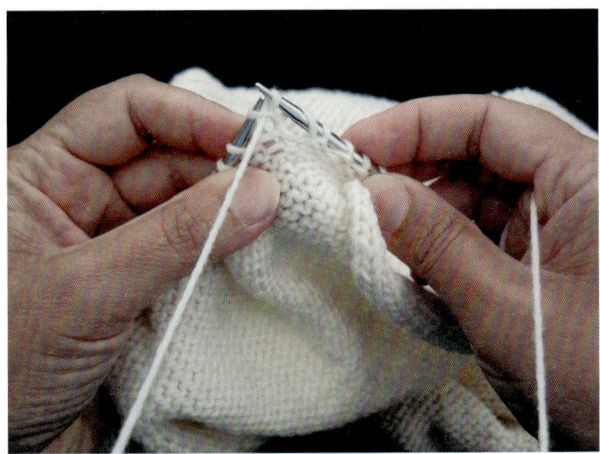

3 Pull the stitch through the loop, away from you and off of the left hand needle.

Purl Through the Back Loop

1 Insert the right hand needle from back to front into the back loop of the stitch.

2 Wrap the yarn around the right hand needle counterclockwise.

3 Pull the stitch through the loop...

4 ...and toward the back.

The Knit Stitch

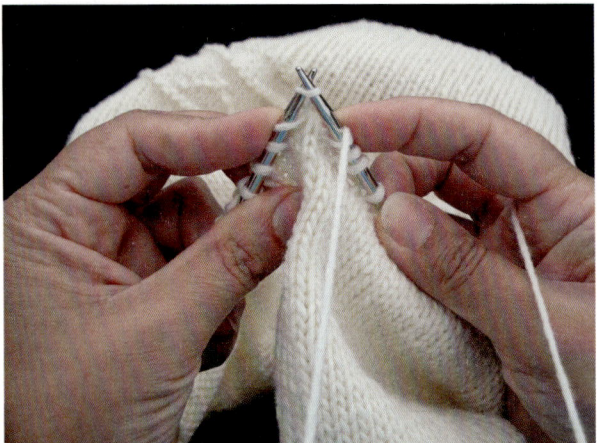

Important note: The working yarn should be on top of (behind) your right hand needle to start to knit. Either dive the right hand needle under the working yarn or slip the first stitch as if to knit on every row.

1 Insert the right hand needle as if to knit in the front loop of the next stitch. Do this by crossing the right hand needle in front (or on top) of the left hand one in one single motion.

2 Using your left thumb, wrap the working yarn around the tip of the right hand needle counterclockwise or from the top down.

3 Pull the stitch through the loop toward you moving the right hand needle from right to left of the loop. Drop the stitch from the left needle.

Knit Through the Back Loop

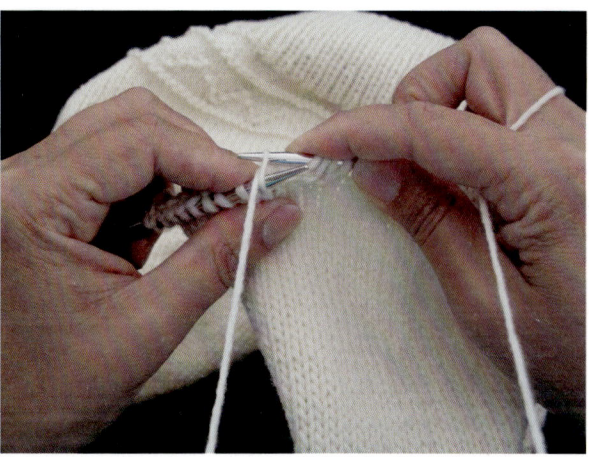

1. Insert the right hand needle into the back loop of the next stitch on the left hand needle.

2. Using your left thumb, bring the yarn all the way to the back around the tip of the right hand needle.

3. Scoop the yarn toward you or toward the front and at the same time through the back loop.

Ribbing

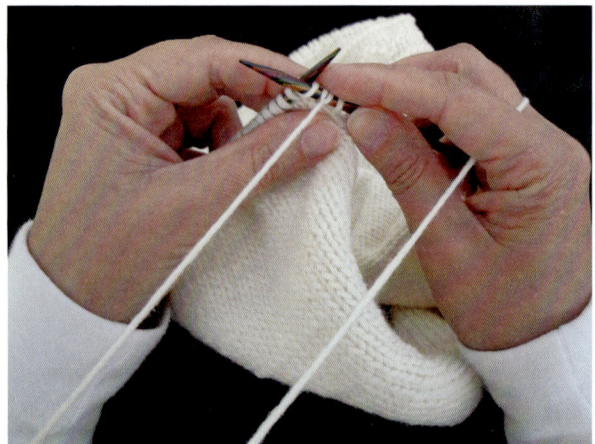

1. In order to knit, the working yarn has to be on top of or behind the right hand needle. Then insert the right hand needle as if to knit.

2. Wrap the yarn around the right hand needle counterclockwise.

3. Finish the knit stitch by pulling the yarn through the loop toward you and off the left hand needle.

4. Use your left thumb to bring the yarn into position to purl.

The Basic Technique—Ribbing

 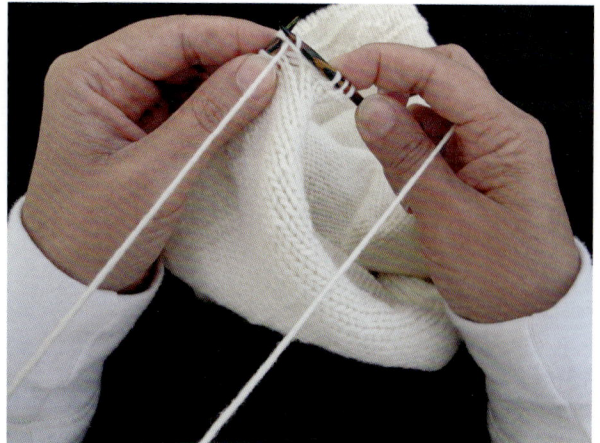

5 Insert the right hand needle as to purl. Wrap the yarn counterclockwise around the top of the right hand needle.

6 Pull the stitch through the loop and away from you, toward the back of the work. When it's time to knit again, use your left thumb to elevate the working yarn a little bit, then dive the right needle under it. Repeat from step 1 to produce a knit one, purl one ribbing.

Increases
Yarn over between two knit stitches

1 Knit the first stitch normally. Yarn is on top of right hand needle.

2 Bring the yarn from the top of the right hand needle to below the right hand needle

The yarn over is the simplest increase there is. It will create a hole in your fabric that is often desirable for decoration as in lace work.

3 Knit the next stitch producing an automatic yarn over.

The Basic Technique—Increases: Yarn Over

Yarn over between two purl stitches

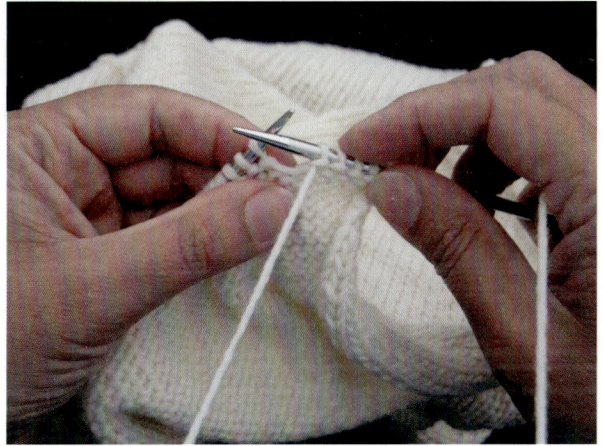

1 Purl the first stitch normally.

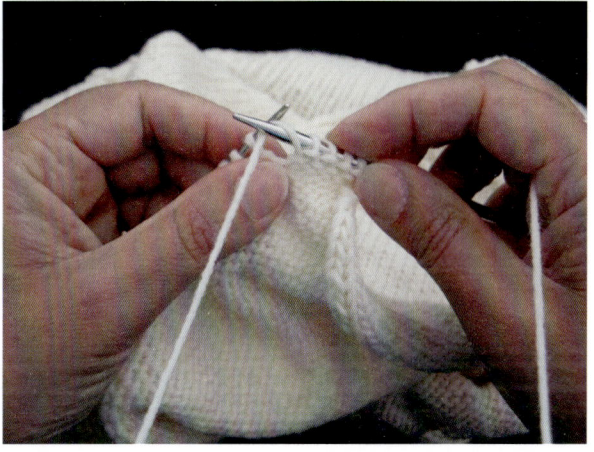

2 Using your left thumb, wrap the yarn counterclockwise around the right hand needle once.

3 Purl the next stitch.

Lifted increase to the right (mirror image of left)

1 Knit first in the right leg of the stitch that is below the stitch on the left hand needle.

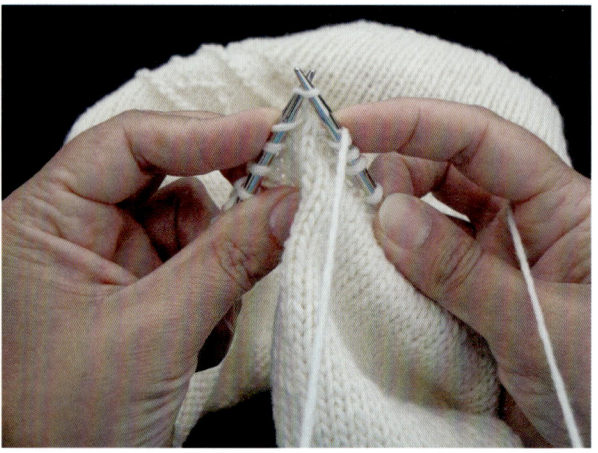

2 You may prefer to put the leg on the left needle and knit it.

3 Move the yarn to the space between the needles with your left thumb.

4 Then knit in the stitch on left hand needle.

Lifted increase to the left (mirror image of right)

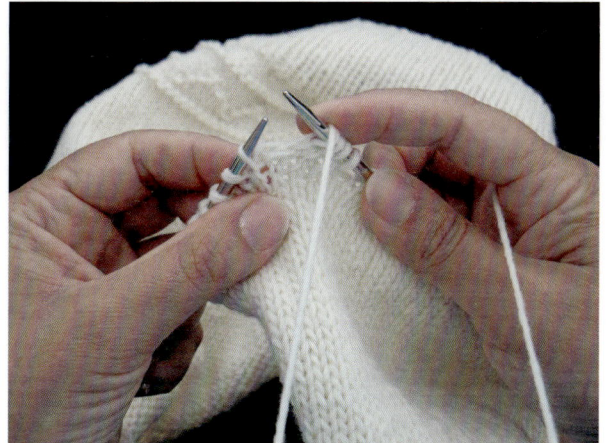

1 Knit in the stitch on the left hand needle.

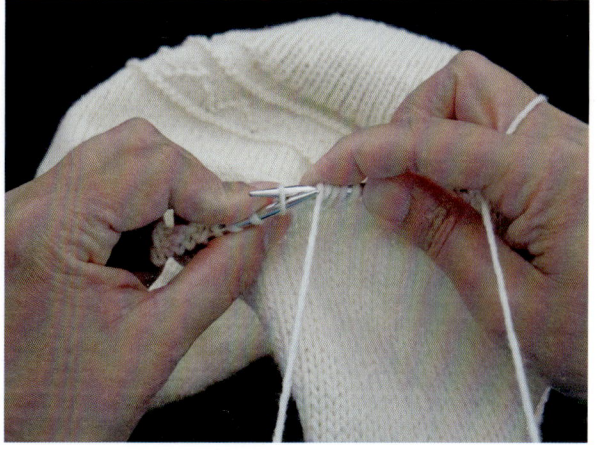

2 Pick up the left leg of the stitch two rows below the one you just worked on.

3 Put this leg on the left hand needle.

4 Knit it through the back loop.

Portuguese Style of Knitting

*Knit in the front and in the back of the stitch—
Method #1*

1. Insert right needle into stitch in the Portuguese knitting position.

2. Bring the yarn between needles with left thumb.

3. Pull the yarn through the left stitch but do not drop it from the left hand needle.

4. Bring your right hand needle and working yarn toward the back loop.

The Basic Technique—Increases: Knit front and back of stitch

5 Insert your right hand needle into the back loop as the picture shows and knit it through the back loop.

6 With this method you end up with a purl bump under the second stitch.

Knit in the front and in the back of the stitch—Method #2

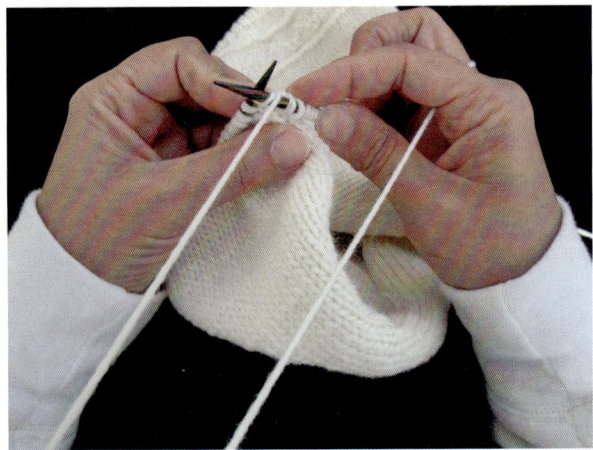

1 I find this method more pleasing because a purl does not show. As before, knit the stitch through the front loop.

2 Do not drop it from the left hand needle.

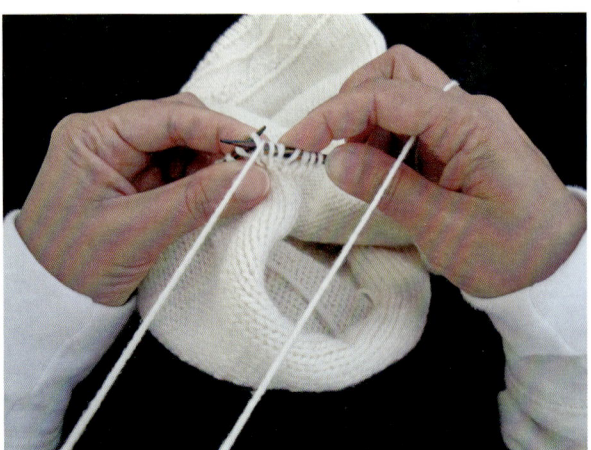

3 Now insert the right hand needle into the same stitch as if to purl and drop it off of the left hand needle. Done!

In this picture you can compare both ways and decide for yourself which one you like better.

The Basic Technique—Increases: Knit front and back of stitch, Make one

Make-one increase (M1)—Half-hitch loop

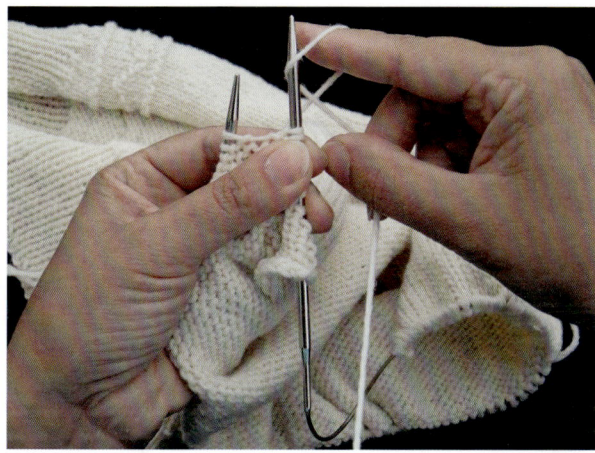 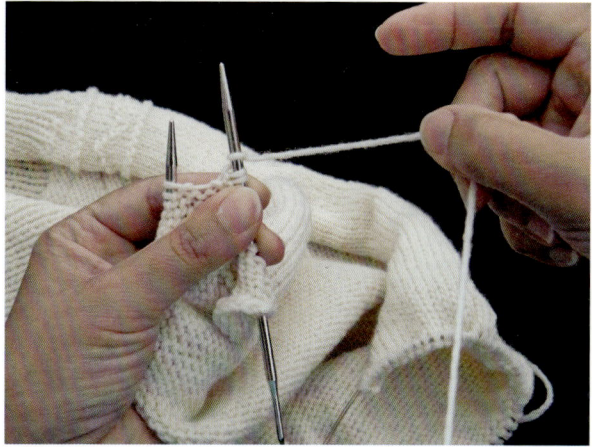

1 Make a loop around the right hand needle as with a loop or half-hitch cast on.

2 Twist the loop so it doesn't form a yarn over when you knit into it.

Make-one increase (M1)—Twisted bar

1 Pick up the strand between two stitches to make the loop.

2 Twist the loop so it doesn't form a yarn over. Knit in the twisted loop.

The Basic Technique— Increases: Make one, Decreases: k2tog, p2tog

Decreases—*Knit two together*

1 Insert right needle as if to knit one stitch Portuguese style, but catch two loops together. Move yarn between needles with left thumb.

2 Pull the stitch through and drop the two stitches off of the left needle.

Purl two together

1 Insert right needle as you would to purl one stitch Portuguese style, but catch two loops together. Move yarn between needles with left thumb.

2 Pull the stitch through and drop the two stitches off of the left needle.

33

Portuguese Style of Knitting

SSK (slip, slip, knit)

1 Insert right needle into stitch as if to knit that stitch. Slip the stitch off of the left onto the right needle.

2 Repeat Step 1 with next stitch.

3 Insert the tip of the left needle into the two stitches you just slipped. As you do this, catch the working yarn in the crossing of the two needles.

4 Using your left thumb, move the working yarn behind the tip of the right hand needle.

The Basic Technique—Decreases: ssk

5 Scoop the yarn toward you...

6 ...and off of the left hand needle.

7 Notice that this decrease slants in mirror image to knit two together.

35

Portuguese Style of Knitting

Portuguese Bind Off

The Portuguese bind off relies again on the use of purl stitches. This technique gives a nice and loose but tidy bind off to any project.

In most instances you want a loose bind off, for example on necklines of pullovers, on cuffs, around a lace shawl, or even when you bind off sleeve caps. It's a very simple bind off to teach beginners.

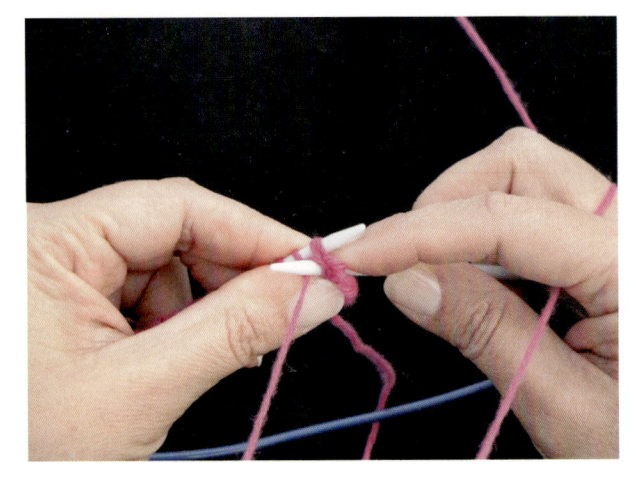

1 *Purl 2 stitches together.

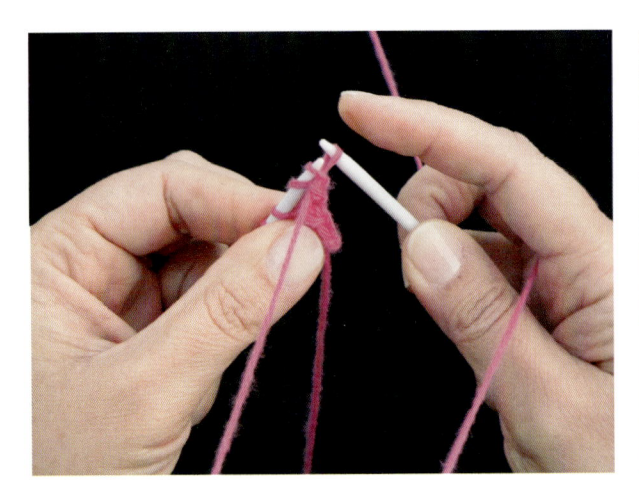

2 This leaves one stitch on your right hand needle. Move this stitch back onto the left hand needle.

3 Repeat from * for the total number of remaining stitches to be bound off.

Advanced Techniques

Once you know how to cast on, bind off, work knit and purl stitches, increase and decrease, you know the basic techniques of knitting.

Now let's see how I work other techniques in knitting. Of course they all rely on the basics, but in some of them you can see a particular way of doing it Portuguese style. If you have previous experience knitting Fair Isle, cables, lace, or entrelac, you will see exactly where the differences are or where it would be done the same way no matter what style.

Knitting with Two Colors

In the past, I combined two knitting styles when knitting with two colors of yarn per round. I carried the main color around my neck and I held the background color Continental style in my left hand. Recently I challenged myself to wear two knitting pins (one on each shoulder) and tension the yarn around each pin. I kept track of which color was on what pin because that determined which color goes over and which goes under—or which color is dominant and which color is background. In the Portuguese style of knitting, the dominant color is the one that goes over the background color.

To set up, choose which color is going to go around the pin on your left shoulder and which one is going to go on your right shoulder. The dominant color depends upon if you work with the knit side facing or the purl side facing. *Once you determine that, do not change it until the project is done.* The yarns come from the work, up around the pins toward the outer side of your body and around fingers on both hands.

Portuguese Style of Knitting

Working two-color knitting with knit side facing

When you have the knit side facing you, the dominant color will be at your left shoulder and the background color on your right shoulder.

When knitting with two different colors in the same round, the unused color will strand at the back of your work. If one of these strands floats behind the work for more than 3 stitches (depending on your gauge), the strand could be snagged. One way to avoid this is by trapping the colors as they travel on the non-public side of the work. The technique for trapping changes depending upon which side of the work is facing you—knit side or purl side. It also changes depending upon whether you need to trap the main color or the background color.

How to trap main color with knit side facing

1 Insert the right hand needle as if to knit in the next stitch.

2 Wrap the gray yarn (main color—MC) over the needle as if to knit.

3 Also wrap the purple yarn (background color—BC) over as if to knit.

Advanced Techniques—Two-color knitting, Trap main color on knit side

4 Unwrap the gray yarn (MC) out of the way.

5 Complete the stitch using the purple (BC). Work one extra stitch (or more) in purple (BC) to complete the trap.

This picture shows the gray (MC) trapped in the back of the work

Portuguese Style of Knitting

How to trap background color with knit side facing

1 Knit up to the stitch where you want to trap the background color. Insert the right hand needle as if to knit.

2 Bring the purple (BC) over the gray (MC) and behind the right hand needle.

3 Wrap the gray (MC) as if to knit.

4 Unwrap the purple (BC) using your left thumb.

Advanced Techniques—Two-color knitting, Trap background color on knit side

5 Complete the knit stitch in gray (MC).

6 Knit one more stitch in gray (MC) to complete the trapping.

This picture shows you the purple (BC) trapped in the back of the work.

Portuguese Style of Knitting

Working two-color knitting with purl side facing

When you purl, the dominant (main) color comes from your right shoulder and the background color comes from your left shoulder. The main color still crosses over the background color.

How to trap main color with purl side facing

1 Insert the right hand needle as if to purl on the next stitch.

2 Bring the red (MC) yarn over and behind the right hand needle.

3 Wrap the yarn as if to purl using the white color (BC).

Advanced Techniques—Two-color knitting, Trap main color on purl side

4 Take the red (MC) out of your way unwrapping the yarn.

5 Complete the stitch by purling it with white (BC). Complete trapping of red (MC) by purling the next stitch in white (BC).

This picture shows you the red color trapped among the white stitches on the back of the work.

Portuguese Style of Knitting

How to trap background color with purl side facing

1 Insert the right hand needle as if to purl.

2 Wrap the white (BC) as if to purl.

3 Wrap the red (MC) as if to purl.

4 Unwrap the white (BC) using your left thumb.

Advanced Techniques—Two-color knitting, Trap background color on purl side

5 Complete the stitch using red (MC).

6 Work one extra stitch in red to complete trapping.

This picture shows you the white color (BC) trapped among red stitches.

Portuguese Style of Knitting

Cables

In this example, I have a six-stitch cable—crossing three stitches over (or under) three stitches. Count the sequence of stitches from the right: 1-2-3-4-5 and 6. I'll knit 4-5-6 first then 1-2-3 either behind or in front of stitches 4-5-6.

1 Insert your right hand needle into the fourth stitch as if to knit.

2 Knit this stitch.

3 As I pull this stitch off the left hand needle, I drop stitches 1, 2 and 3 temporarily.

Advanced Techniques—Cables

4 Slip the three stitches (1, 2, and 3) onto the left needle and finish knitting stitches 5 and 6.

5 Now knit the three stitches that were held behind the work.

6 Check to make sure the cable crosses the proper direction.

Portuguese Style of Knitting

Double Knitting

Double knitting is a form of knitting where two fabrics are produced simultaneously with two yarns and one pair of knitting needles (straight or circular). The two fabrics may be connected or not.

When would you use double knitting? You might choose double knitting when you knit a pocket on a sweater or when you want to line a mitten for extra warmth. Producing garment and lining at the same time avoids sewing and finishing it later.

When working using two colors of yarn in double knitting patterns, each square of the chart represents two stitches and the pattern is reversible. If you are knitting a motif from a chart, the same motif is worked on both sides at the same time but the colors are reversed. For any chart you follow you have to work with double the number of stitches. Divide them in pairs: the first stitch of the pair is knitted and will produce the fabric that is closer to you; the second stitch of the pair is purled and will produce the fabric that is away from you. You can either cast on the right number of stitches and double it later or cast on double.

Many of my students claim that ribbing, brioche stitch and double knitting when worked Portuguese style has a rhythm that makes the work easier and more pleasant. Again, it requires less maneuvering of your hands when you work with the yarn available in front of the work at all times.

For detailed information about the technique I recommend the book *Double Knitting: Reversible Two-Color Designs* by M'Lou Baber.

1 Start with both colors on top of right hand needle to knit the first stitch of a pair.

2 Insert the right hand needle as to knit.

Advanced Techniques—Double knitting

3 Knit the first stitch of the pair.

4 Move both colors of yarn below the right hand needle and insert it as if to purl into the second stitch of the pair.

5 Purl the second stitch.

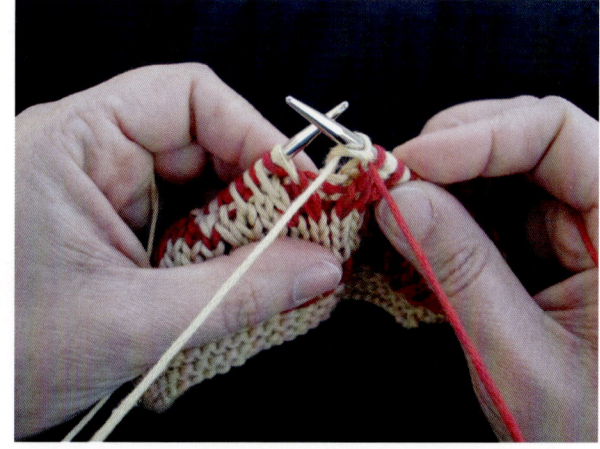

6 Both stitches correspond to one square of the chart and you just finished a pair.

Portuguese Style of Knitting

The Advantages of Working with Hooked Needles

When I spent time with Portuguese knitters and observed them knitting with hooked knitting needles, I understood why they like it so much.

First, when working on a circular project while using a set of five hooked needles, two hooks never face each other so that the hook helps you make the stitch.

Second, the hook also makes it easier to work in the opposite direction for short rows, bobbles and entrelac without turning.

The third advantage of using a hooked knitting needle is to bind off stitches as crochet.

I use interchangeable needles so that I can decide where I want the hook and where I want the knitting needle to be. For binding off as crochet I have the hooked needle in my right hand. For the knitting from the right needle to the left, I keep the hooked needle in my left hand.

Binding off as crochet

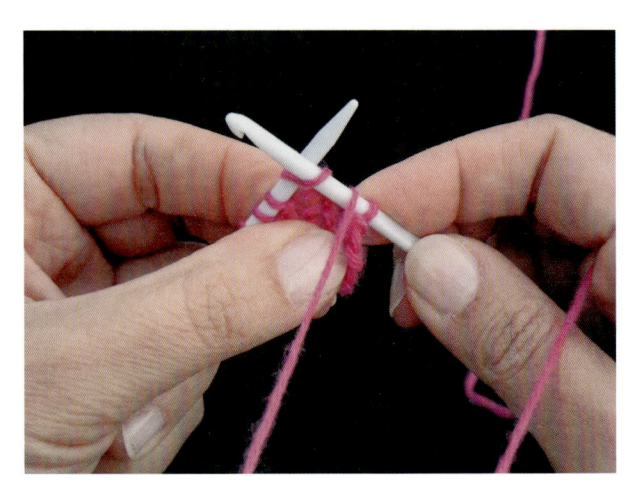

1 Insert hooked needle as if to knit.

2 Knit one stitch regularly.

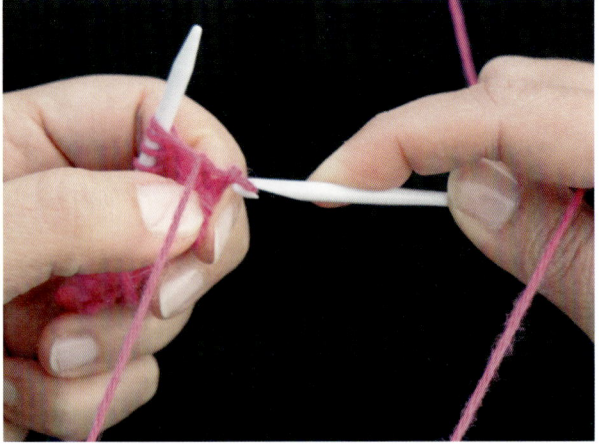

3 Knit a second stitch and pull this stitch through the loop and through the first stitch as well. Repeat for as many stitches as you want to bind off.

Advanced Techniques—Binding off as crochet, Working with hooked needles

Knitting from the right needle to the left needle

1 Insert left hand needle (hooked) behind the right one.

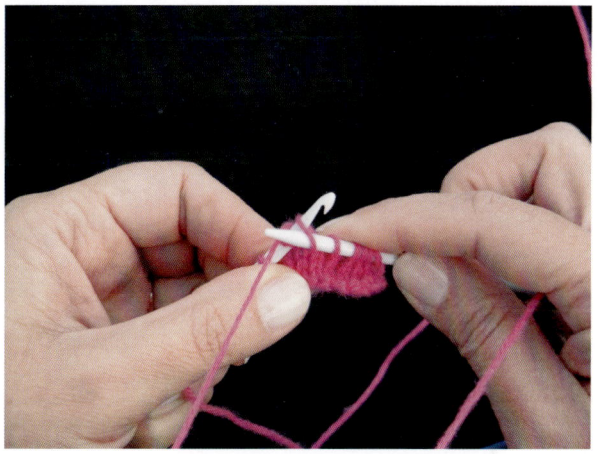

2 Wrap the yarn counterclockwise using your right thumb (from top down).

3 Pull the stitch through the loop and toward you as you move the hook from right to left.

4 Pull the stitch off of the right hand needle.

❈ Portuguese Spinning ❈

These are old pictures of Portuguese women using their spindles
—Courtesy of Tita Costa

The spindles at the left are examples of the tools these spinners might have used.

Portuguese Style of Knitting

Even though this is not the subject of my book, I know many of my readers are also spinners. They and other fiber enthusiasts will enjoy learning a little bit about the Portuguese spinning and spindles. I have done a brief research on the subject and found very little. This might open the doors for you to continue seeking information.

The Portuguese spinner holds the spindle with her right hand continuously twisting the top of it and holds the fiber with her left hand (some women keep the fiber in a pocket). The spinner pulls her hands apart and never lets the spindle drop, which makes the process different and less frustrating than using the drop spindle.

Depending on the region they are from, the Portuguese spindles vary from completely carved in wood to having the top part made out of metal. The very top of the spindles (either carved or metal) have a spiral-shaped groove like a wide screw spiral. The weight of the spindle is very important, and women choose the one that feels best in their hands. The length of the carved spindles can vary between 9 and 12.5 inches. They are made of heather wood. These come from the mountains, and are still being made but, with the forest fires, the desired size of heather wood is getting scarce. The metal spindles are no longer made.

Tita Costa (on right) and a group of Portuguese knitters get together once a month for updates on their projects. Their friendship and expertise are keeping these crafts and traditions alive in Portugal. Note the Portuguese spindle on the table and in her hand.

❈ Portuguese-Inspired Patterns ❈

Cloud Mittens and Scarf – page 58

Juliana's Baby Sweater – page 62

Manuela Scarf – page 66

Traditional Fisherman Sweater – page 69

Portuguese Style of Knitting

Sidewalk Mosaic Headband – page 84

Rooster Mittens – page 76

Traditional Socks – page 80

Cascais Woman's Vest – page 86

Design Inspiration

I have designed ten projects inspired by the Portuguese culture to share with you a little bit of what I know about it, and to give you a chance to practice the techniques I describe in this book. My sources of inspiration include textiles, architectural details, paving stones, monuments, churches, icons, and the lovely tiles of Moorish influence.

Abbreviations

General:

k – knit

p – purl

garter stitch – purl every row. If you decide to knit every row, read *knit* where it says *purl*.

exchange stitch join – place the first stitch you cast on beside the last stitch you cast on (needle points will be facing each other). Bring the first stitch from your left hand needle to your right hand needle. Now, bring the last stitch you cast on from your right hand needle to the left one, passing it over the first stitch.

St(s) – stitch(es)

RS – right side

WS – wrong side

rep – repeat

Increases:

yo – yarn over

M1R – make one stitch to the right. Insert left needle point, from back to front, under the horizontal bar joining the last stitch on the right needle to the first stitch on the left needle. Knit through the front of the loop.

M1L – make one stitch to the left. Insert left needle point, from front to back, under the horizontal bar joining the last stitch on the right needle to the first stitch on the left needle. Knit through the back of the loop.

Decreases:

ssk – slip, slip, knit 2 tog through back loop.

k2tog – knit 2 stitches together

p2tog – purl 2 stitches together

Cables:

CF4 – (cross cable 2X2 to front) slip next 2 sts to cable needle and hold in front, knit following 2 sts, return sts from cable needle to left hand needle and knit them.

CF6 – (cross cable 3X3 to front) slip next 3 sts to cable needle and hold in front, knit following 3 sts, return sts from cable needle to left hand needle and knit them.

CB4 – (cross cable 2X2 to back) slip next 2 sts to cable needle and hold in back, knit following 2 sts, return sts from cable needle to left hand needle and knit them.

CB6 – (cross cable 3X3 to back) slip next 3 sts to cable needle and hold in back, knit following 3 sts, return sts from cable needle to left hand needle and knit them.

Chart key

Read the charts from bottom to top. When knitting in the round, read each row of the chart right to left. When knitting back and forth, read the odd numbered rows right to left and even numbered rows left to right.

☐ knit on right side (RS); purl on wrong side (WS)

⊡ purl on RS; knit on WS

⊻ slip with yarn to RS

⊙ yo

⊠ k2tog   ⊠ ssk

▱ sl 1, k2, pass slipped stitch over (psso)

▱▱ CF4

▱▱ CF6

▱▱ CB4

▱▱ CB6

Cloud Mittens and Scarf

Nuvens: luvas e cachecol

This scarf and mitten set is fairly simple to knit. The scarf is knitted on two needles, back and forth while the mittens are knitted in the round—a traditional method. The yarn choice makes these garments comfortable, light and fluffy as a cloud.

Specifications

Size: women's medium
Finished Measurements: Mittens: hand circumference 7.25" (18.5 cm); Scarf: 50"
Materials: 5 skeins of Cascade Yarn, Cloud 9 (50% merino wool/50% angora) 109 yards (100m) each/50 g, or Sublime Angora Merino (80% extra fine merino/20% angora) 130 yards (119 m) each/50 g
Gauge: 23 stitches = 4" (10 cm) over stockinette
Needles: set of US 5 (3.75 mm) double pointed needles for mittens, and US 5 (3.75 mm) straight or circular for scarf
Experience Level: intermediate
Skills: experience with double pointed needles and making cables

Mitten

Cuff

Cast on 42 sts using long-tail cast on distributing stitches as follows:

11 sts on needle #1
21 sts on needle #2
10 sts on needle #3

Join work in the round, being careful not to twist cast-on row. Work in ribbing 1x1 (knit 1 st, purl 1 st) for 18 rounds or 2.5" (6.5 cm), or desired length from cast on edge. Then work *Right-hand thumb gusset* for the right mitten or *Left-hand thumb gusset* for the left mitten.

Right-hand thumb gusset

Needle #1: knit across;
Needle #2: follow the *Back-of-Hand Chart*;
Needle #3: k1 and place a safety pin on this stitch (it's going to be the center stitch between increases from now on) and k to end.

Cloud Mittens and Scarf

Round 1:

Needle #1: knit across;

Needle #2: follow the *Back-of-Hand Chart*;

Needle #3: increase 1 st before the marked stitch (M1L) and another after the marked stitch on Needle #3 (M1R), knit to end of round.

You now have 44 sts.

Round 2:

Needle #1: knit across;

Needle #2: follow the *Back-of-Hand Chart*;

Needle #3: knit across.

Repeat rounds 1 and 2 until you have 13 sts on thumb gusset (your center stitch plus 6 sts on each side of it), and 54 sts total.

Chart key

Read the charts from bottom to top. If you are knitting in the round, read each row of the chart right to left. If you are knitting back and forth, read the odd numbered rows right to left and even numbered rows left to right.

☐ knit on right side (RS); purl on wrong side (WS)

• purl on RS; knit on WS

⊻ slip with yarn to RS

⊠ k2tog

⊠ ssk

▷◁ CF4

◁▷ CB4

▷▷◁◁ CB6

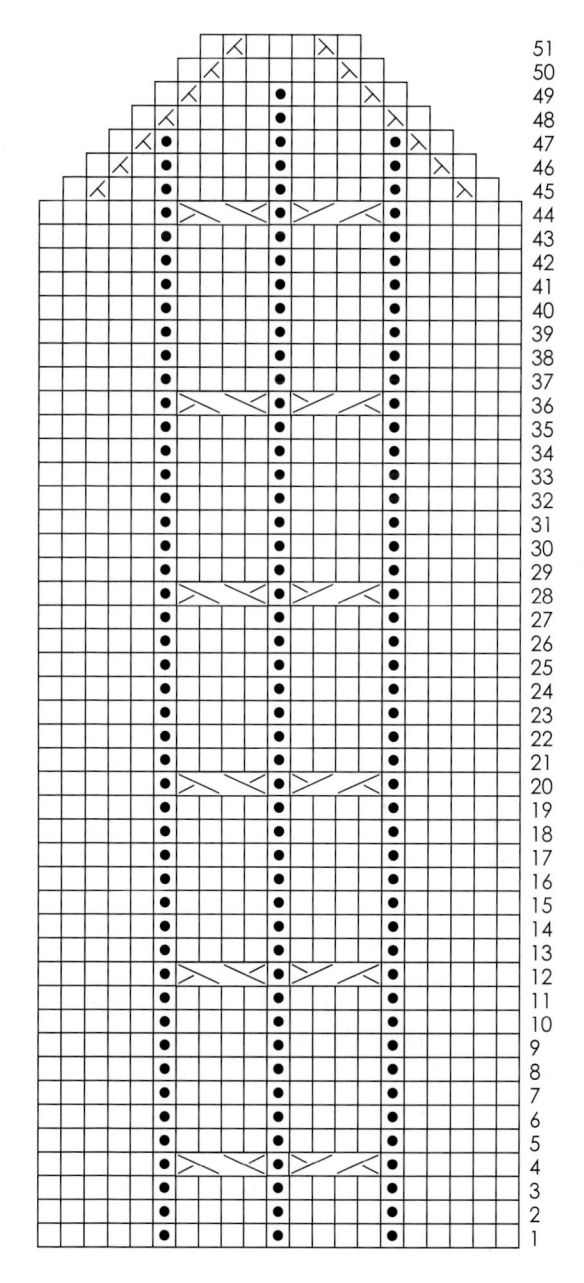

Back-of-Hand Chart

Portuguese Style of Knitting

13 stitches of the thumb gusset are ready to put on hold.

Next round:

Needle #1: knit across;

Needle #2: follow the *Back-of-Hand Chart*;

Needle #3: knit sts for thumb gusset and put these 13 sts on a piece of yarn, then knit to end of round. You now have 41 sts.

Next round:

Where sts are on hold, cast on 1 st by using cable cast on or knitted cast on. You now have 42 sts.

Left-hand thumb gusset

Needle #1: k10, k1 and place a safety pin on this stitch (it's going to be the center stitch between increases from now on);

Needle #2: follow the *Back-of-Hand Chart*;

Needle #3: knit across.

Round 1:

Needle #1: k10, increase 1 st before the marked stitch (M1L) and another after the marked stitch (M1R);

Needle #2: follow the *Back-of-Hand Chart*;

Needle #3: knit across. You have 44 sts.

13 thumb-gusset stitches are on hold on waste yarn.

Round 2:

Needle #1: knit across;

Needle #2: follow the *Back-of-Hand Chart*;

Needle #3: knit across.

Repeat rounds 1 and 2 until you have 13 sts on thumb gusset (your center stitch plus 6 sts on each side of it), and 54 sts total.

Next round:

Needle #1: k10, knit sts for thumb gusset and put these 13 sts on a piece of yarn;

Needle #2: follow the *Back-of-Hand Chart*;

Needle #3: knit across. You now have 41 sts.

Next round:

With sts on hold, cast on 1 st by using cable cast on or knitted cast on. You now have 42 sts. Continue with the rest of the mitten pattern *Above the thumb*.

Above the thumb

Continue knitting all rounds in established pattern until mitten is 8" (20.5 cm) from beginning.

Cloud Mittens and Scarf

Using waste yarn to hold thumb-gusset stitches allows flexibility to continue knitting the hand.

Decrease for top of mitten

Try mitten on recipient's hand. It should be even with the top of little finger. Continue cable pattern on back of hand if desired (see chart) as you shape top of mitten over the next 8 rounds.

Decrease as follows:

Needle #1: knit to last 3 sts, k2tog, k1;

Needle #2: ssk, work across to last 3 sts, k2tog, k1;

Needle #3: ssk, knit to end. You have 38 sts.

Repeat this decrease every round until there are 14 sts remaining. Cut yarn, leaving an 8" (20.5 cm) tail. Thread tapestry needle with tail and graft the mitten top using Kitchener stitch.

Thumb

Place 13 sts on hold onto 2 double pointed needles. Using a third needle pick up 1 st in the corner of the thumb, pick up 2 sts at the top of the opening where you cast on, pick up 1 st in the other corner (total of 17 sts). Work in the round. Knit 10 rounds or until thumb length covers half of the thumb nail.

Decrease for Top of Thumb

Round 1: *k3, k2tog; repeat from * to last 2 sts, end k2. You have 14 sts.

Round 2: *k2, k2tog; repeat from * to last 2 sts, end k2. You have 11 sts.

Round 3: *k1, k2tog; repeat from * to last 2 sts, end k1. You have 8 sts remaining.

Cut yarn leaving a 5" (12.5 cm) tail. Using a tapestry needle, run yarn through all remaining stitches and pull it tight. Darn all ends.

Scarf

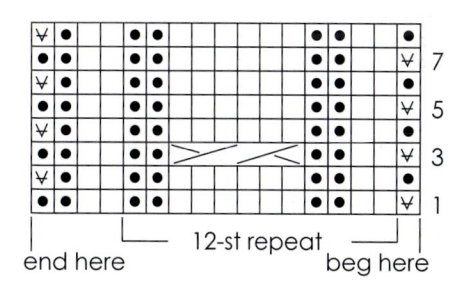

Cast on 54 sts and work in garter stitch for 6 rows (3 ridges).

Row 1 (RS): slip 1, p1, *k2, p2, k6, p2; repeat from * 3 more times, k2, p2.

Row 2 (WS): slip 1, k1, *p2, k2, p6, k2; repeat from * 3 more times, p2, k2.

Rows 3, 5, 7: repeat row 1.

Row 4: slip 1, p1,*k2, p2, CB6, p2; repeat from * 3 more times, k2, p2.

Rows 6, 8: repeat row 2.

Repeat these 8 rows until scarf is 48" (122 cm) long or desired length. End after row 4.

Work in garter stitch for 6 rows (3 ridges). Bind off all 54 stitches loosely.

Juliana's Baby Sweater
Juliana: casaquinho de bebe

*This sweater is worked in one piece, from side to side using short rows.
If you knit Portuguese style, just purl every row.
You start the sweater at the left front edge, work your way around the body,
then finish with the right front, which will overlap the left front.*

Specifications

Sizes: newborn (6, 9) months—chest about 17 (19, 20)"/43 (48.5, 51) cm

Finished Measurements: Chest: 17 (19, 20)"/43 (48.5, 51) cm; Length: 10 (10.75, 11.5)"/25.5 (27.5, 29) cm

Materials: 4 (4, 4) skeins of Sunday Best by Reynolds (51% cotton, 49% viscose, 1.75 oz [50 g], 145 yards [133 m] each)

Gauge: 29 sts and 53 rows = 4" (10 cm) in garter stitch

Needles: size US 2 (2.75 mm) or size to obtain gauge. Crochet hook C/2 (2.75 mm)

Notions: stitch holders and ribbon or four baby buttons (optional)

Experience Level: intermediate

Skill: short rows

Left Front

Cast on 12 sts.

Row 1: purl.

Row 2: purl 2, make 1, purl to last 2 stitches, make 1, purl 2; 2 sts increased.

Repeat these 2 rows 23 (25, 27) more times until you have 60 (64, 68) sts.

Continue increasing 4 more times at the neck edge only (left edge on right side rows). On the bottom edge, continue working straight, without increasing. You have 64 (68, 72) sts. Work 18 (22, 24) rows in garter stitch; 9 (11, 12) ridges.

Row 1: purl 50 (54, 56) sts, leave 14 (14, 16) sts unworked, turn.

Row 2: purl back to bottom edge.

Row 3: purl 57 (61, 64) sts, leave 7 (7, 8) sts unworked, turn.

Row 4: purl back to bottom edge.

Row 5: purl all sts, turn.

Row 6: purl back to bottom edge.

Purl these 6 rows 5 (6, 7) more times.

Left Sleeve

* Purl as follows: purl 50 (54, 56) sts, leave 14 (14, 16) sts unworked, turn and purl 10 (12, 12) sts. Cast on 50 (54, 58) sts for the left sleeve. Place remaining 40 (42, 44) sts on holder. You have 74 (80, 86) sts in work.

Continue working the neck edge in short rows pattern as established and purl short rows at cuff as follows: purl to the last 11 sts of the cuff every other time you reach the cuff edge. When you have a total of 24 (27, 30) ridges on the left cuff, bind off the 50 (54, 58) sts you had cast on for the sleeve, then purl to the end of row (it should be a row 6 of pattern repeat, and you'll end at the neck edge)*.

The photo below shows the left front and the left sleeve including the stitches on the holder.

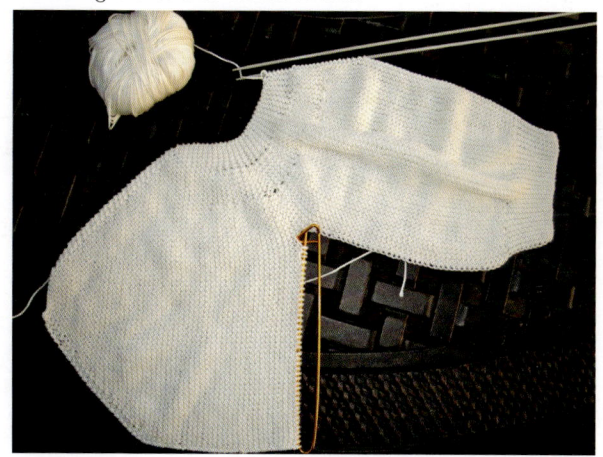

Portuguese Style of Knitting

Back
With RS facing, slip the sts from holder back to the working needle. You have 64 (68, 72) sts in work.

Purl short row pattern rows 1 - 6 19 (21, 22) more times.

Right Sleeve
Work same as for left sleeve from * to *.

Right Front
With RS facing, slip the sts from holder back to working needle. You have 64 (68, 72) sts in work. Purl rows 1 - 6 of short row pattern 6 (7, 8) more times.

I mark a short row (row 3 of each repeat) with safety pins for easier counting.

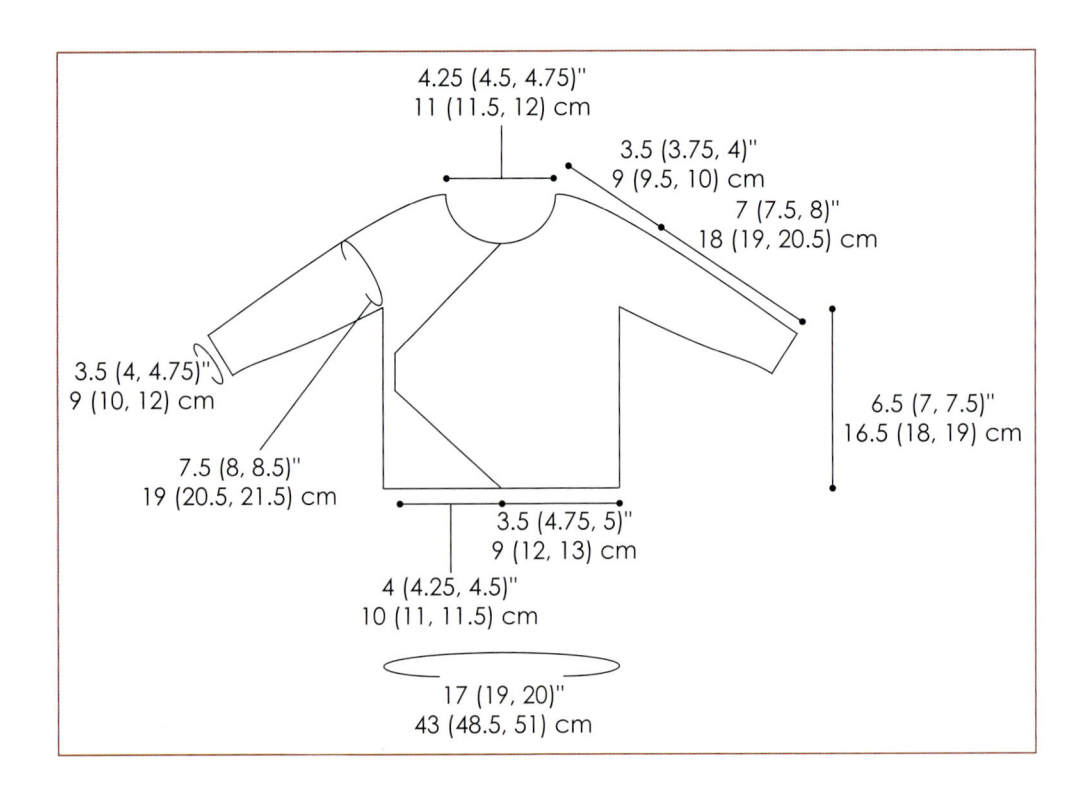

Work 10 (12, 16) rows of garter stitch without short rows; 5 (6, 8) ridges. End at the neck edge.

Decrease for right front:

Row 1: purl 2, p2tog, purl to end; 1 st decreased.

Row 2: purl.

Repeat these 2 rows 3 more times. You have 60 (64, 68) sts.

Decrease on both edges:

Row 1: purl 2, p2tog, purl to last 4 sts, p2tog, purl 2; 2 sts decreased.

Row 2: purl.

Repeat these 2 rows 23 (25, 27) more times. You have 12 sts left. Bind off.

Finishing: with RS facing, pick up and knit 80 (88, 102) sts around neck edge. Work 3 rows in garter stitch.

Next row (RS): make buttonhole as follows, knit 2, k2tog, yo, knit to end.

Work 2 more rows in garter stitch.

Bind off all sts.

Sew sleeve seams. Sew button to left end of neck band and ribbon at the pointed edges at the front as shown.

Optional: On the white version of this sweater, instead of a neck band, I did 1 row of single crochet around the outer edges of body and neck, and put 4 crochet loops at the left front for buttonholes. Buttons were sewn to the side of the right front under the buttonholes.

The Lisbon Sé Cathedral, built on the site of a Saracen mosque in the 12th century, features many treasures such as the font where Saint Anthony of Padua was baptized, and numerous relics, images and icons.

❈ Manuela Scarf ❈
Cachecol da Manuela

As I observed the Manueline architecture in Lisbon, I was inspired to design this scarf. This pattern has a 3X3 cable and a simple lace that is easy to memorize and fun to knit!

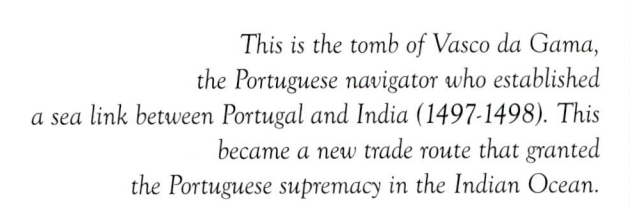

It was here at the site of "Mosteiro dos Jeronimos" that Vasco da Gama and his men spent the night before going on his voyage for India in 1497. Manuel I started this construction to celebrate that successful journey. It was meant to be a place for the burial of the Aviz Dynasty but also became a house of prayer for the seamen.

This is the tomb of Vasco da Gama, the Portuguese navigator who established a sea link between Portugal and India (1497-1498). This became a new trade route that granted the Portuguese supremacy in the Indian Ocean.

Manuela Scarf

Specifications

Size: one size fits all

Finished Measurements: about 6.25" (16 cm) x 54.75" (139 cm)

Materials: 3 skeins of Qiviuk (45% qiviuk, 45% extra fine merino wool and 10% silk) by Jacques Cartier Clothier (Size 2/14, 1 oz [28 g], 217 yards [199 m] each)

Gauge: 45 stitches = 4" (10 cm) over pattern

Needles: size US 3 (3.25 mm), 24" long circular or straight needles

Experience Level: intermediate

Skills: cables and lace

Using size US 3 needles and the Portuguese cast on, cast on 71 sts. Work 12 rows in reverse garter stitch (purl every row); 6 ridges total.

Row 1 (RS): p7, [k2, yo, k5, k2tog, p2, k6, p2] 3 times, p7.
Row 2 (WS): p7, [k2, p6, k2, p2tog, p6, yo, p1] 3 times, p7.
Row 3: p7, [k3, yo, k4, k2tog, p2, k6, p2] 3 times, p7.
Row 4: p7, [k2, p6, k2, p2tog, p5, yo, p2] 3 times, p7.
Row 5: p7, [k4, yo, k3, k2tog, p2, CF6, p2] 3 times, p7.
Row 6: p7, [k2, p6, k2, p2tog, p4, yo, p3] 3 times, p7.
Row 7: p7, [k5, yo, k2, k2tog, p2, k6, p2] 3 times, p7.
Row 8: p7, [k2, p6, k2, p2tog, p3, yo, p4] 3 times, p7.
Row 9: p7, [k6, yo, k1, k2tog, p2, k6, p2] 3 times, p7.
Row 10: p7, [k2, p6, k2, p2tog, p2, yo, p5] 3 times, p7.
Row 11: p7, [k9, p2, k6, p2] 3 times, p7.
Row 12: p7, [k2, p6, k2, p9] 3 times, p7.
Row 13: p7, [k2, yo, k5, k2tog, p2, CF6, p2] 3 times, p7.

The ancient Saint Anthony chapel in the Manueline style was panelled in gilded wood carvings in the 17th century.

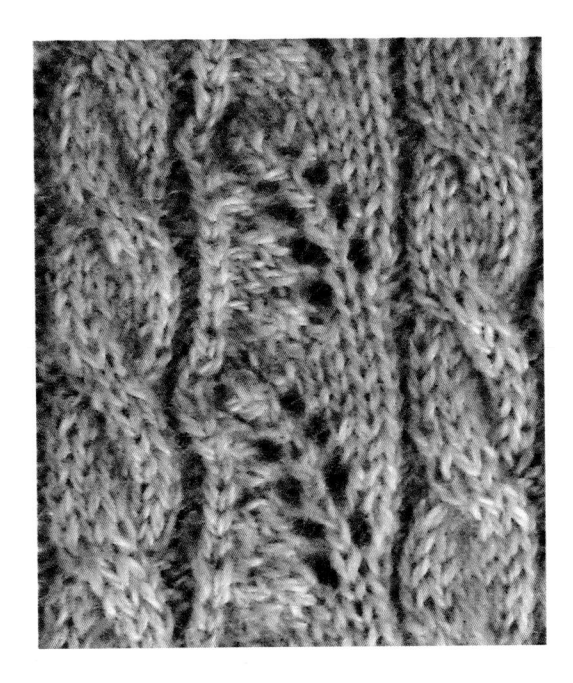

Portuguese Style of Knitting

Row 14: p7, [*k2, p6, k2, p2tog, p6, yo, p1] 3 times, p7.
Row 15: p7, [k3, yo, k4, k2tog, p2, k6, p2] 3 times, p7.
Row 16: p7, [k2, p6, k2, p2tog, p5, yo, p2] 3 times, p7.
Row 17: p7, [k4, yo, k3, k2tog, p2, k6, p2] 3 times, p7.
Row 18: p7, [k2, p6, k2, p2tog, p4, yo, p3] 3 times, p7.
Row 19: p7, [k5, yo, k2, k2tog, p2, k6, p2] 3 times, p7.
Row 20: p7, [k2, p6, k2, p2tog, p3, yo, p4] 3 times, p7.
Row 21: p7, [k6, yo, k1, k2tog, p2, CF6, p2] 3 times, p7.
Row 22: p7, [k2, p6, k2, p2tog, p2, yo, p5] 3 times, p7.
Row 23: p7, [k9, p2, k6, p2] 3 times, p7.
Row 24: p7, [k2, p6, k2, p9] 3 times, p7.

Repeat rows 1-24 until scarf measures 54" (137 cm) or desired length.

Work 12 rows in reverse garter stitch (purl every row) or 6 ridges total.

Bind off all stitches loosely. Block scarf.

Chart key

Read the charts from bottom to top. Since you are knitting back and forth, read the odd numbered rows right to left and even numbered rows left to right.

☐ knit on right side (RS); purl on wrong side (WS)
● purl on RS; knit on WS
○ yo
⊠ k2tog on right side, p2tog on wrong side
⋈ CF6

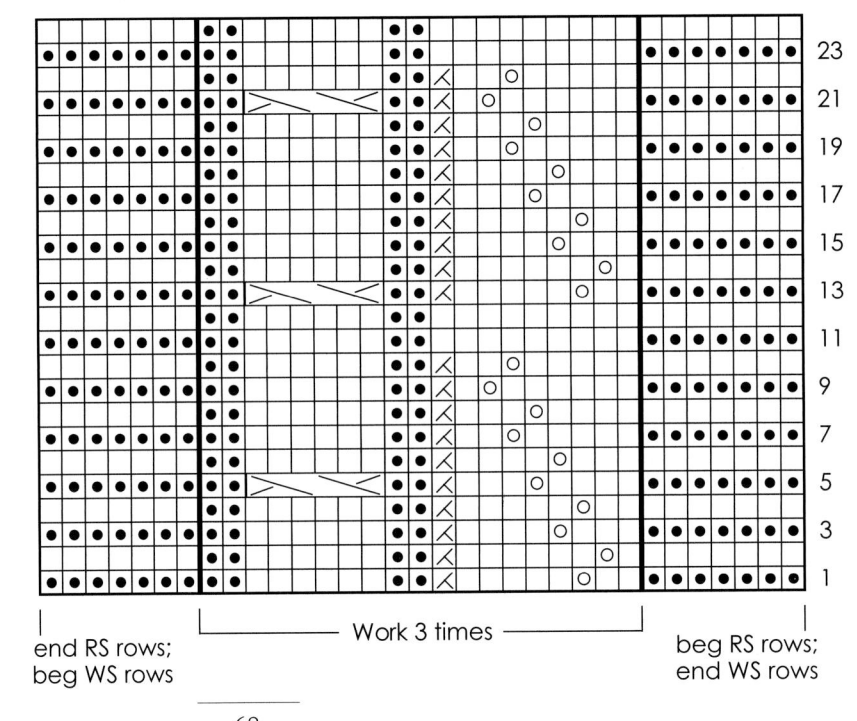

Traditional Fisherman Sweater
Malha de Pescador Tradicional

The traditional Portuguese sweater is knitted in natural off-white color and then embroidered using black and red yarn and cross-stitch nautical motifs.

Specifications

Sizes: men's small (medium, large, extra large)

Finished Measurements:

Chest: 40 (43.5, 47.5, 51.5)"/101.5 (110.5, 120.5, 131) cm

Length: 25.5 (26, 26.5, 27)"/65 (66, 67.5, 68.5) cm

Materials: 11 (12, 13, 13) skeins of 8-ply Treliske Organic Merino (100% unbleached undyed organic merino wool) 110 yds (101 m) each/50g

Gauge: 22 sts and 32 rows = 4" (10 cm) in St st; 22.5 sts and 36 rows = 4" (10 cm) in pattern

Needles: size US 6 (4 mm) straight or circular needle, and double pointed needles, or size to obtain gauge

Notions: stitch holders, safety pins, 11" (28 cm) zipper, and waste yarn for provisional cast on

Experience Level: intermediate

Skills: knit and purl

Front

Using straight or circular needle and long-tail cast on, cast on 100 (108, 118, 130) sts. Work in ribbing 1X1 (knit 1 st, purl 1 st) for 2.5" (6.5 cm), end with a WS row.

Next row: Change to stockinette stitch. Increase 10 (12, 14, 14) sts evenly along the first row; 110 (120, 132, 144) sts.

Work 3 more rows of stockinette.

Work Chart 1 on page 72.

Continue in stockinette stitch until piece measures 15.5 (16, 16, 16.5)"/39.5 (40.5, 40.5, 42) cm from cast on edge, end with a WS row. Place a safety pin on each side edge to mark armholes. Divide work at center of row for right and left front.

Next row: k1 (3, 3, 3), begin as shown for your size and work Chart 3 on page 73 for left front, attach a separate ball of yarn, and work Chart 2 on page 73 for right front, ending as shown for your size, k1 (3, 3, 3).

Continue first 1 (3, 3, 3) st(s) and last 1 (3, 3, 3) st(s) in stockinette stitch, and charts as established until armhole measures 10 (10, 10.5, 10.5)"/25.5 (25.5, 26.5, 26.5) cm. Place all stitches on holders.

Back

Using straight or circular needle and long-tail cast on, cast on 100 (108, 118, 130) sts. Work in ribbing 1X1 for 2.5" (6.5 cm), end with a WS row.

Next row: change to stockinette stitch. Increase 10 (12, 14, 14) sts evenly along the first row; 110 (120, 132, 144) sts.

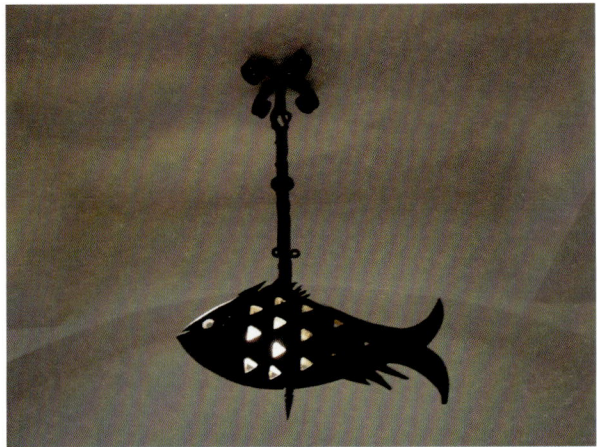

Work 3 more rows of stockinette.

Work Chart 1 on page 72.

Continue in stockinette stitch until piece measures 15.5 (16, 16, 16.5)"/39.5 (40.5, 40.5, 42) cm from cast on edge, end with a WS row, and increase 1 st at center of last row; 111 (121, 133, 145) sts.

Place markers 46 (51, 57, 63) sts from edges, with 19 sts at center of back between markers.

Next row: k1 (3, 3, 3), work Chart 6 on page 74 for right back, Chart 5 on page 72 for 19 center sts, and Chart 4 on page 74 for left back, k1 (3, 3, 3); begin and end charts as shown for your size.

Continue first 1 (3, 3, 3) st(s) and last 1 (3, 3, 3) st(s) in stockinette stitch, and charts as established until piece measures 10 (10, 10.5, 10.5)"/25.5 (25.5, 26.5, 26.5) cm from beginning of charts. Leave sts on needle.

Place all sts from right front on a circular needle. Hold needles with WS together and join 36 (41, 46, 50) sts at each shoulder, starting at armhole and using 3-needle bind off.

Repeat for left front and back.

Many sights in Portugal reveal the close ties between the Portuguese people and the sea. These pavement and statuary displays on the Belem waterfront commemorate the explorers who participated in voyages of discovery.

Collar

Using circular or double pointed needles and with RS facing, knit the remaining 19 (19, 20, 22) sts from right front, knit the 39 (39, 41, 45) sts from center back and decrease 1 st at the center of back, then knit the remaining 19 (19, 20, 22) sts from left front: 76 (76, 80, 88) sts.

Work back and forth in stockinette stitch for 5 more rows. Change to garter stitch and work another 8 rows. Leave all stitches on the needle.

Sleeves (knit two)

Using straight or circular needles and long-tail cast on, cast on 62 (66, 70, 72) stitches. Work in ribbing 1X1 for 3" (7.5 cm), end with a WS row.

Change to stockinette stitch and work 4 rows. Work Chart 1. Knit 1 row and increase 1 st at each end; 64 (68, 72, 74) sts.

Continue stockinette stitch and *at same time* increase 1 st at each end every 6 rows 23 (14, 18, 14) times, then every 8 rows 0 (7, 4, 7) times; 110 (110, 116, 116) sts. When sleeve measures 22.5"/57 cm from cast on edge for all sizes, bind off all stitches.

Finishing

Block pieces. Sew sleeves to body between safety pins marking armholes. Sew side seams.

I-cord finish for collar: using double pointed needles, cast on 3 sts using waste yarn. Change to your working yarn and knit 1 row. Slide all stitches to other end of needle without turning.

Next row: * knit 2, slip 1, pick up 1 stitch from the collar and knit these 2 together (the slipped stitch and the one from the collar) through the back loop; slide sts without turning and repeat from * until all collar stitches have been worked.

Continue working I-cord to fit around front opening, picking up loops of edge sts as you work. When the I-cord reaches the waste yarn, graft ends together. Sew zipper into front opening.

Portuguese Style of Knitting

Chart key

Read the charts from bottom to top. When knitting back and forth, read the odd numbered rows right to left and even numbered rows left to right.

☐ knit on right side (RS); purl on wrong side (WS)

● purl on RS; knit on WS

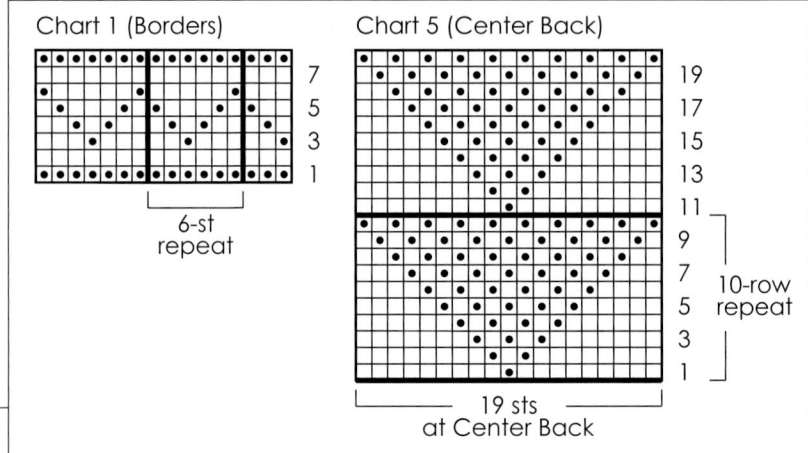

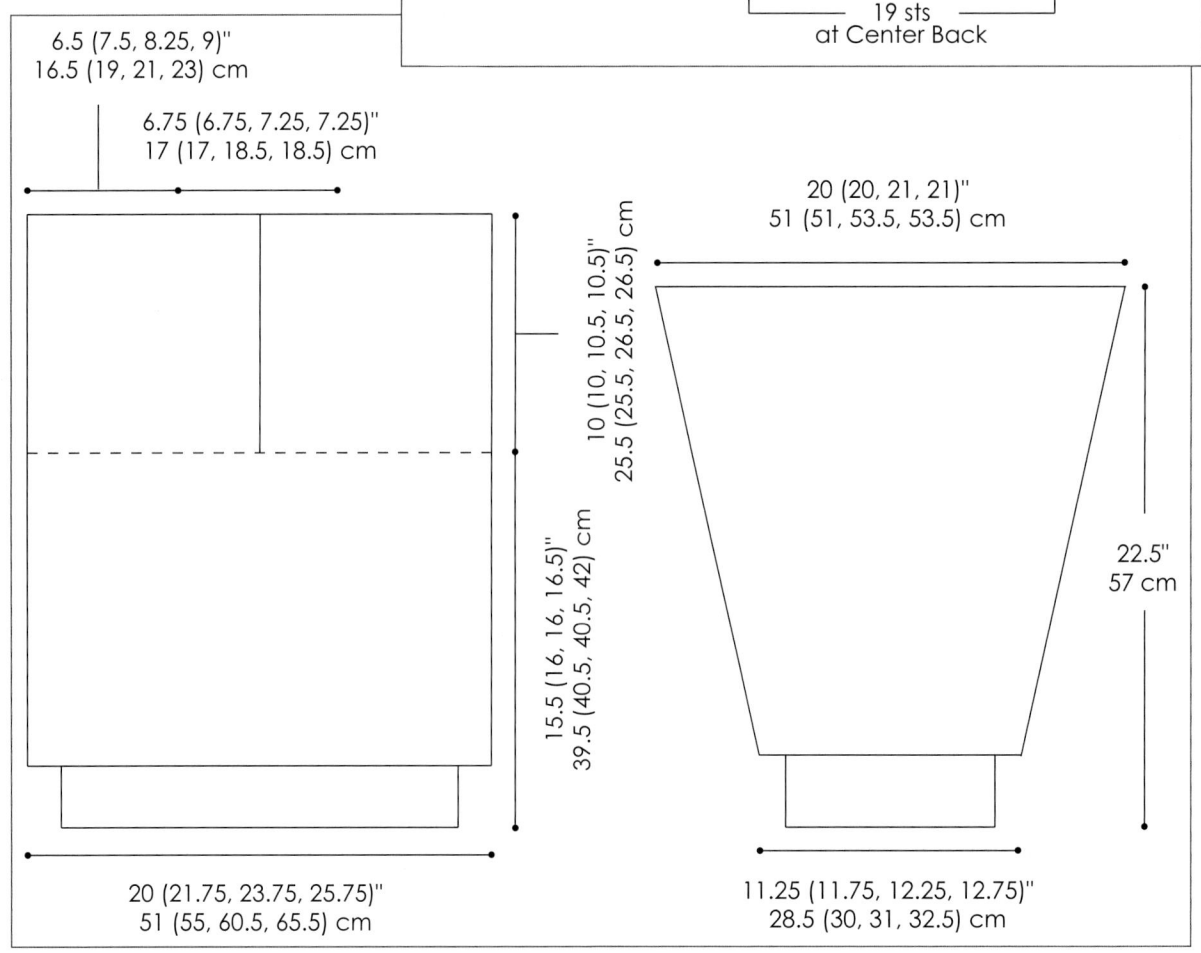

Chart 1 (Borders)

6-st repeat

Chart 5 (Center Back)

19 sts at Center Back

10-row repeat

6.5 (7.5, 8.25, 9)"
16.5 (19, 21, 23) cm

6.75 (6.75, 7.25, 7.25)"
17 (17, 18.5, 18.5) cm

10 (10, 10.5, 10.5)"
25.5 (25.5, 26.5, 26.5) cm

15.5 (16, 16, 16.5)"
39.5 (40.5, 40.5, 42) cm

20 (20, 21, 21)"
51 (51, 53.5, 53.5) cm

22.5"
57 cm

20 (21.75, 23.75, 25.75)"
51 (55, 60.5, 65.5) cm

11.25 (11.75, 12.25, 12.75)"
28.5 (30, 31, 32.5) cm

Traditional Fisherman Sweater

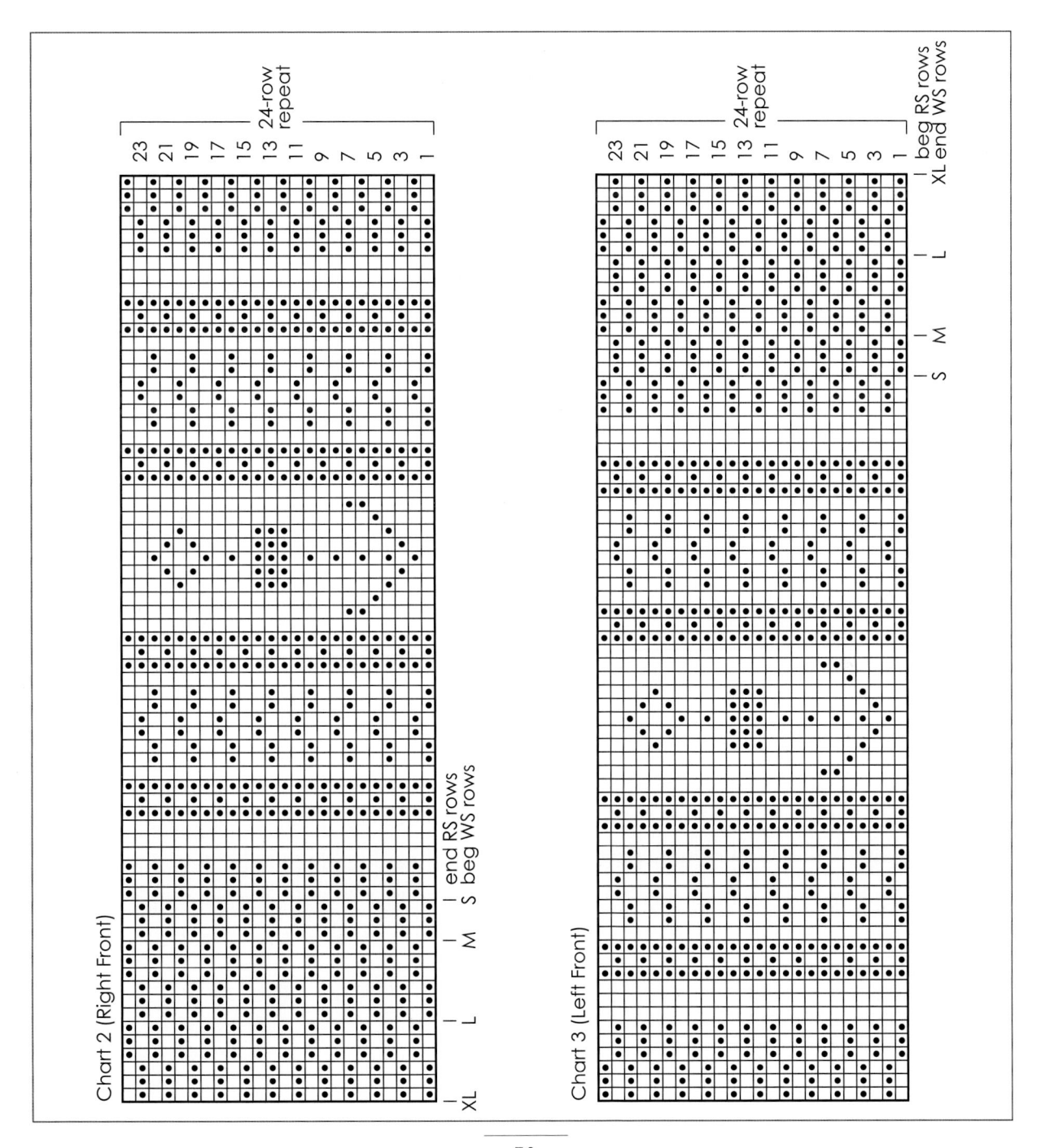

Chart 2 (Right Front)

Chart 3 (Left Front)

Portuguese Style of Knitting

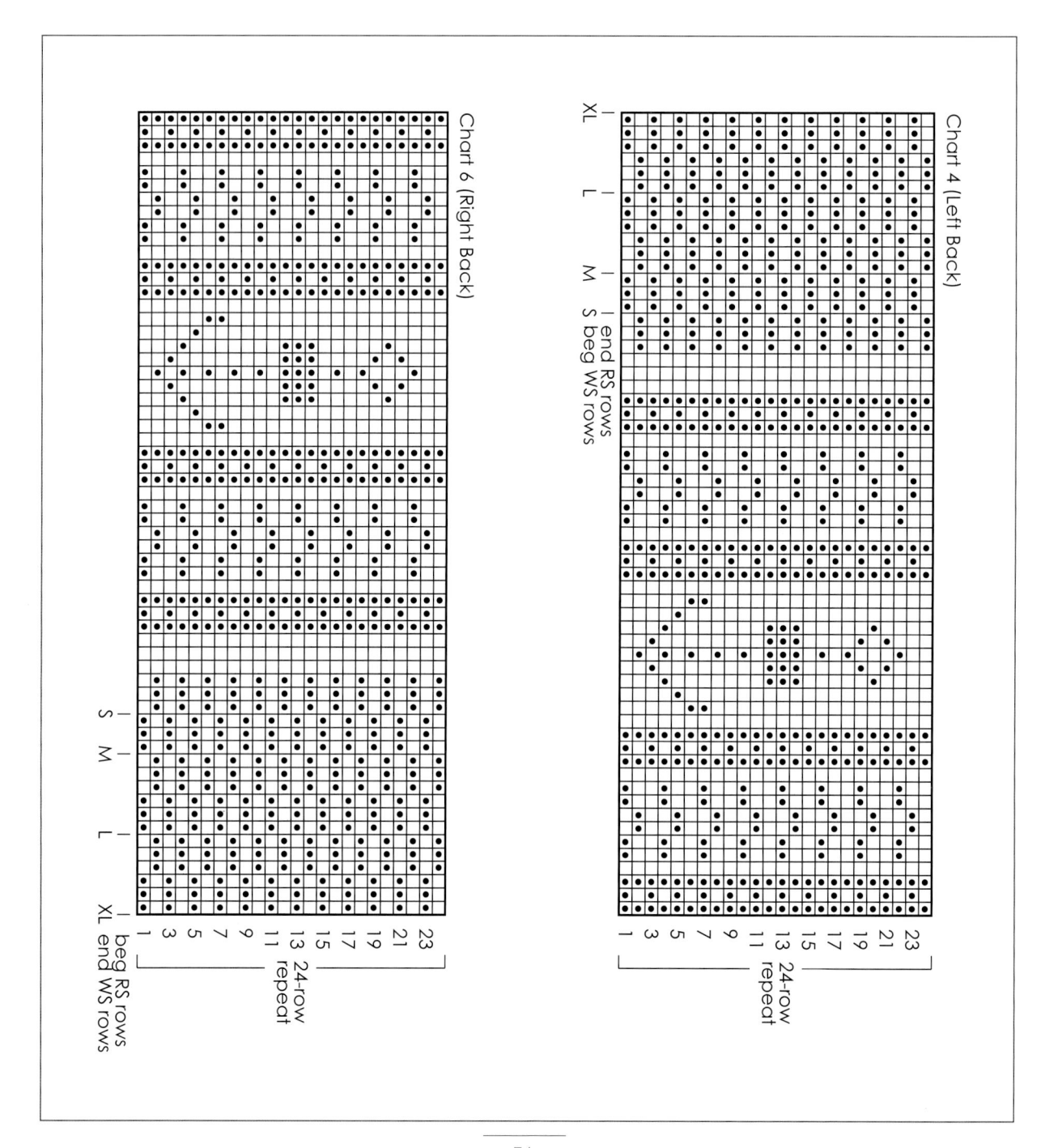

Chart 4 (Left Back)

XL — L — M — S — beg WS rows / end RS rows

Rows: 1, 3, 5, 7, 9, 11, 13, 15, 17, 19, 21, 23

24-row repeat

Chart 6 (Right Back)

S — M — L — XL — beg RS rows / end WS rows

Rows: 1, 3, 5, 7, 9, 11, 13, 15, 17, 19, 21, 23

24-row repeat

Traditional Fisherman Sweater

These folk sweaters are hand knit using wool in natural off-white color. After they are knitted, they are embroidered with cross-stitch motifs in black and red colors—the crown, ducks, anchors, nautical instruments, acronyms, crossed oars, etc. Initially they were embroidered by retired men who worked in wool all of the symbols of their lives. In time, they were made by women—mothers, wives, fiancées of the fishermen. Part of the masculine costume for parties and processions, these sweaters have their origins in the early nineteenth century.

Photo is courtesy of Tracy Holroyd-Smith

Portuguese Style of Knitting

The color-change patterns on the cuff and surrounding the rooster are inspired by tile designs that are so prevalent in Portugal. The pattern on the palm of the mitten is Brazilian. These mittens are re-sized by changing yarn weight and needle size.

Rooster Mittens
Luvas de Barcelos

The Barcelos Rooster is an unofficial tourist symbol in Portugal. It signifies honesty, good fortune and honor. Its origin is unknown but variations of the legend abound. This legend is associated with carvings on an antique stone cross in the city of Barcelos, Portugal. The pictures on the cross show the Virgin Mary, St. Paul, the sun, the moon and a dragon on one side of the stone. On the other is Christ crucified, a rooster, and St. James holding a hanging man. According to the legend, an unknown thief stole a piece of silver during a banquet hosted by a wealthy man in Barcelos. Although nobody knew who stole the silver, the authorities arrested a pilgrim who was on his way to St. James of Compostella. Although he protested that he was innocent, nobody believed him. He was convicted and sentenced to death.

On the day of his execution, he asked to be taken to the judge who had passed the sentence. His request was granted, and the hangman took him to the house of the judge, who was dining with some friends. The pilgrim again protested his innocence, asked for the intercession of St. James and then pointed at a roasted chicken on the table. He exclaimed, "If I am innocent, that cock will crow when I am hanged." Everybody laughed at him as he was taken away to be hanged.

During the hanging, the cock stood up on the table and crowed. No one any longer doubted the innocence of the condemned man so he was immediately released and sent on his way. The legend says that pilgrim returned and erected the stone cross to commemorate the event.

77

Specifications

Size: women's small (medium, large)
  Hand circumference: 7 (7.5, 8)"/18 (19, 20.5) cm
  Length: 10 (10.5, 11)"/25.5 (26.5, 28) cm

Materials: fingering weight wool. One skein of each of 3 colors: dark, light and white. Various hues of embroidery floss

Gauge: 34 (32, 30) sts and 40 (38, 36) rounds = 4" (10 cm) over pattern

Needles: size US 0 (2 mm) for size small, US 1 (2.25 mm) for size medium, and US 2 (2.75 mm) for size large, or size to obtain gauge. Different size needles are used for each size

Notions: stitch markers, stitch holders and embroidery needle

Experience Level: intermediate, with stranded knitting experience

Skill: work around with double pointed needles

Right Mitten

Using dark yarn, cast on 60 sts. Join in the round being careful not to twist stitches. Read the chart from right to left every round, and work from bottom to top.

Rnd 1: knit.

Rnd 2: purl.

Rnd 3: with white, knit.

Rnds 4 – 5: *k1, p1; rep from * around.

Rnds 6 – 52: continue following chart for color changes.

Rnd 53: work 31 sts, place next 11 sts for thumb opening on holder, cast on 11 sts in pattern over hole, then continue in pattern to end of rnd. Work through rnd 90, or until hand is about 1" (2.5 cm) short of desired length.

Rnd 91: *k1, ssk, k25 in pattern, k2tog: rep from * once more. 4 sts decreased.

Rnds 92 – 100: Continue decreasing in this manner following the chart for stitch count and color changes.

Distribute remaining sts on two needles, with 10 sts on each needle. Graft sts together using dark color.

Thumb

Knit 11 sts from holder, pick up and knit 1 st at edge of hole, 11 sts in the cast on sts at top of thumb hole, plus 1 st at edge of hole. You have 24 sts.

Join work in the round. Follow the Thumb Chart for color changes until thumb measures about 2" (5 cm), or 0.5" (1.5 cm) short of desired length.

Rnds 21 – 24: work shaping in same manner as top of hand. Gather remaining 8 sts using dark.

Left Mitten

Work left mitten same as right through rnd 52.

Rnd 53: work 49 sts, place next 11 sts for thumb opening on holder, cast on 11 sts in pattern over hole. Continue left mitten same as right.

Finishing

Weave in ends. Wash mitten by hand using cold water and mild soap. Squeeze excess water and let it dry flat.

Embroidery

Using embroidery thread in colors of your choice, chain stitch and duplicate stitch designs on the rooster. Beads can also be used.

Rooster Mittens

(At left) Palm of right mitten.

(Below) Back of mitten without embroidery.

Thumb

Traditional Socks

Meias Rusticas

These socks are very typical of those from the northern part of Portugal. The yarn is hand spun and they use mostly natural wool colors.

Specifications

Size: child's small (child's medium, women's, men's)

Materials: off-white and brown socks: About 400 yards (366 m) of sport yarn (5 oz [140 g]) For this pattern I used traditional hand spun yarn from Serra da Estrela (Portugal).

Gauge: 28 sts and 48 rnds = 4" (10 cm) in stockinette stitch. This is important for accurate sizing

Needles: Size US 2 (2.75 mm) or size to obtain gauge

Experience Level: intermediate

Skill: work around with double pointed needles

Rustic Socks

Cuff

Using long-tail cast on, cast on 44 (52, 60, 64) sts and divide sts onto 3 needles as follows:

Needle #1: 11 (13, 15, 16) sts;

Needle #2: 22 (26, 30, 32) sts;

Needle #3: 11 (13, 15, 16) sts.

Join work in the round being careful not to twist stitches. Use exchange stitch join or cast on an extra stitch, and knit the first and last sts together.

Work ribbing 2X2 (knit 2 sts, purl 2 sts) for 1.5 - 2" (4 - 5 cm).

Next round: *k2tog, yo; rep from * across.

Knit one round.

Next round: *yo, k2tog; rep from * across.

Change to stockinette stitch (knit every round and work for 6 - 7" (15 - 18 cm).

Heel

Slip sts from needle #1 and #3 to the same needle: 22 (26, 30, 32) sts. These will be the heel flap.

Work flat as follows (rib pattern):

Row 1 (RS): *slip 1 as if to purl, k1; rep from * across.

Rows 2 (WS): slip 1 as if to purl, purl to end.

Repeat these 2 rows until heel flap measures about 2 – 2.5" (5 – 6.5 cm).

Turn Heel

With WS facing you, work:

Row 1: p13 (15, 17, 18) sts, p2tog, p1, then turn.

Row 2: slip 1 st as if to purl, k5, ssk, k1, then turn.

Row 3: slip 1, p6, p2tog, p1, then turn.

Row 4: slip 1, k7, ssk, k1, then turn.

Continue working this way until you reach the st before where the heel was turned. Work the next 2 sts together (the st before and the st after the gap), work 1 more st, then turn.

Repeat this row until all the heel sts have been worked, and 14 (16, 18, 18) sts remain.

Heel gusset

Divide remaining heel sts onto 2 needles and knit in the round on 3 needles as follows:

Needle #1: knit sts from Needle #1, then pick up and knit 11 (13, 15, 16) along left side of heel flap;

Needle #2: knit all sts on Needle #2;

Needle #3: pick up and knit 11 (13, 15, 16) sts on the right side of heel flap, and knit remaining sts of heel; 58 (68, 78, 82) sts.

Decrease as follows:

Round 1:

Needle #1: knit across until 3 sts remain, k2tog, k1;

Needle #2: knit across;

Needle #3: k1, ssk, knit to end; 2 sts decreased.

Round 2: knit.

Repeat these 2 rounds 6 (7, 8, 8) more times; 44 (52, 60, 64) sts.

Foot

Keep knitting plain rounds until sock reaches about 0.75 (0.75, 1, 1)" /2 (2, 2.5, 2.5) cm] short of desired length from heel. End having just knit across Needle #3. Distribute sts evenly on 4 needles; 11 (13, 15, 16) sts on each needle.

Spiral Toe

Read through directions for toe before working.

Decrease as follows:

Round 1: *k2tog, knit to end of needle; repeat from * 3 more times.

Round 2: *k1, k2tog, knit to end of needle; repeat from * 3 more times.

Round 3: *k2, k2tog, knit to end of needle; repeat from * 3 more times.

Round 4: *k3, k2tog, knit to end of needle; repeat from * 3 more times.

Round 5: *k4, k2tog, knit to end of needle; repeat from * 3 more times.

Continue in this manner until 8 sts are on each needle. Start with Round 1 again and decrease until 4 sts are on each needle. Start with round 1 again and decrease until 2 sts are on each needle. Cut yarn, leaving a 5" (12.5 cm) tail. Run yarn through remaining sts, pull it tight. Darn in ends.

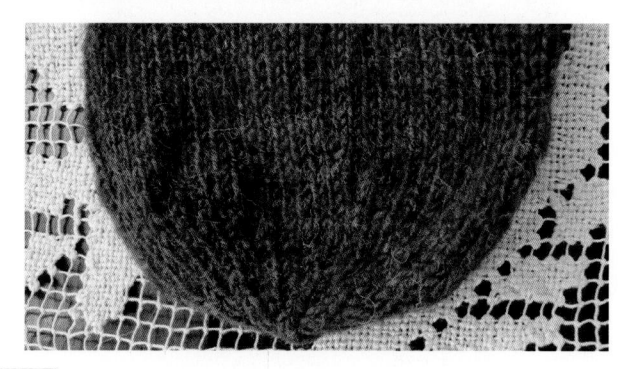

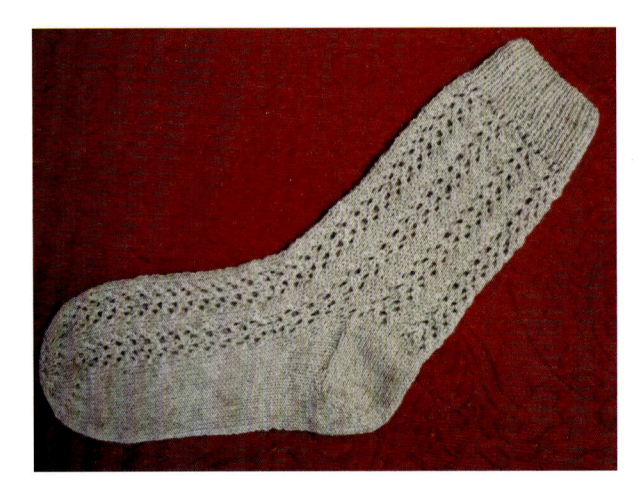

Portuguese Style of Knitting

I decided to design a sock keeping the traditional cuffs, heel and spiral toe of the Portuguese pattern, but adding a lace pattern to make it more feminine.

Specifications

Size: women's medium

Materials: 2 skeins of Lovit Yarn from Fibre-Isle Fine Yarns (Canada) (60% superwash super fine merino, 30% Lyocell cellulose, 10 % premium Canadian bison) 246 yds (225 m) each 50 g

Gauge: 34 sts and 43 rnds = 4" (10 cm) in Lace Pattern

Needles: size US 2 (2.75 mm) or size to obtain gauge

Experience Level: intermediate

Skill: work circularly with double pointed needles

Lacy Socks

Lace pattern (multiple of 8 sts)

Round 1: *k2, k2tog, yo, k1, yo, ssk, k1; repeat from * to end.

Rounds 2 and 4: Knit.

Round 3: *k1, k2tog, yo, k3, yo, ssk; repeat from * to end. Repeat these 4 rounds for pattern.

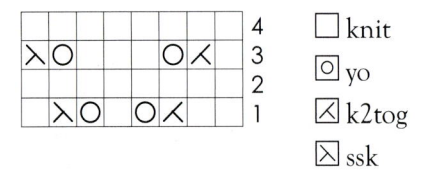

- ☐ knit
- ◯ yo
- ⊠ k2tog
- ⊠ ssk

Cuff

Using long-tail cast on, cast on 64 sts dividing sts onto 3 needles (16, 32, 16 sts).

Join work in the round being careful not to twist stitches. Work in ribbing 1X1 (knit 1 st, purl 1 st) or 2X2 (knit 2 sts, purl 2 sts) for 18 rounds.

Next round: *k2tog, yo*. Repeat from * to * around.

Next round: knit.

Start with round 1 of Lace Pattern and continue until cuff is about 7" (18 cm).

Heel

Slip sts from needle #1 and #3 to the same needle; 32 sts; these will be the heel flap. Working flat as follows (rib pattern):

Row 1 (RS): *slip 1 as if to purl, k1; rep from * across.

Rows 2 (WS): slip 1 as if to purl, purl to end.

Repeat these 2 rows until heel flap measures about 2 – 2.5" (5 – 6.5 cm).

Turn Heel

With WS facing you, work:

Row 1: p18, p2tog, p1, then turn.

Row 2: slip 1 st as if to purl, k5, ssk, k1, then turn.

Row 3: slip 1, p6, p2tog, p1, then turn.

Row 4: slip 1, k7, ssk, k1, then turn.

Continue working this way: work until you reach the st before where the heel was turned, work the next 2 sts together (the st before and the st after the gap), work 1 more st, then turn; repeat this row until all the heel sts have been worked, and 18 sts remain. Heel is turned!

Heel gusset

Divide remaining heel sts onto 2 needles. Now you are back to knitting in the round on 3 needles. Knit sts from Needle #1, pick up and knit 16 sts along left side of heel flap, knit all sts on Needle #2. With Needle #3, pick up and knit 16 sts on the right side of heel flap, then knit remaining sts of heel; 82 sts.

Decrease as follows:

Round 1:

Needle #1: knit across until 3 sts remain, k2tog, k1;

Needle #2: knit across;

Needle #3: k1, ssk, knit to end; 2 sts decreased.

Round 2: knit.

Repeat these 2 rounds 8 more times; 64 sts.

Keep knitting plain rounds until sock reaches about 1" (2.5 cm) short of desired length from heel. End having just knit across Needle #3. Distribute sts evenly on 4 needles; 16 sts on each needle.

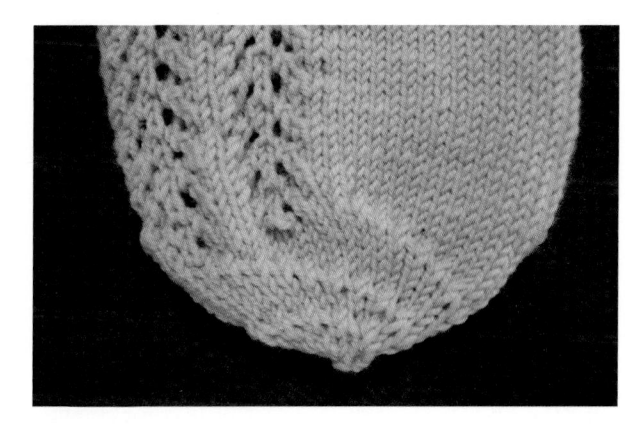

Spiral Toe

Read through directions for toe before working.

Decrease as follows:

Round 1: *k2tog, knit to end of needle; repeat from * 3 more times.

Round 2: *k1, k2tog, knit to end of needle; repeat from * 3 more times.

Round 3: *k2, k2tog, knit to end of needle; repeat from * 3 more times.

Round 4: *k3, k2tog, knit to end of needle; repeat from * 3 more times.

Round 5: *k4, k2tog, knit to end of needle; repeat from * 3 more times.

Continue in this manner until you have 8 sts left on each needle. Start with round 1 again and decrease until you have 4 stitches on each needle, then start with round 1 again and decrease until you have 2 sts on each needle.

Cut yarn leaving a 5" (12.5 cm) tail. Run yarn through remaining sts, pull it tight, darn ends.

Sidewalk Mosaic Headband
Calçadas de Lisboa, Bandana

Double Knitting

When working double knitting patterns, each square of the chart represents two stitches, and the pattern is reversible; in this pattern, the same motif is worked on both sides but the colors are reversed. Knit the first stitch of the pair with the color shown in the chart while holding the unused color to the back of your work, then purl the second stitch of the pair with the other color, holding the unused strand to the front of your work.

To work the chart, read it as follows: For light squares, knit the first stitch of the pair with Color A, then purl the second stitch of the pair with Color B. For dark squares, knit the first stitch of the pair with Color B, then purl the second stitch of the pair with Color A.

Specifications

Size: women's medium (18"/45.5 cm circumference)

Materials: 2 skeins of Wool Cotton by Rowan (50% merino, 50% cotton – 50 g/123 yards [112 m] each): Color A, #951 Tender, and Color B #903 Misty

Needles: size US 4 (3.5 mm) needles or size to obtain gauge

Gauge: 20 sts and 26 rounds = 4" (10 cm) in pattern

Experience Level: advanced

Skill: double knitting

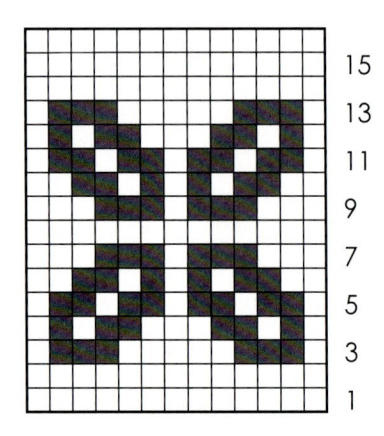

☐ knit with Color A, purl with Color B
■ knit with Color B, purl with Color A

The image below is the view of the knitting as you work. The predominantly darker bands on page 85 are the inside of the knitting as you work.

84

Sidewalk Mosaic Headband

Holding 2 strands of Color A together, cast on 90 sts. Join work in the round being careful not to twist stitches.

Work ribbing 1X1 (knit 1 st, purl 1 st) for 5 rounds then increase 1 st; 91 sts. Cut 1 strand of Color A and join Color B.

Alternate Colors A and B in both loops of each stitch as follows:

*Knit first loop of next st using Color A and purl the second loop of same stitch using Color B (one pair of sts worked); rep from * around. The number of stitches doubled to 182.

Work 16 rounds of the pattern chart.

Cut Color B, leaving a tail about 6" (15 cm) long. Using Color A, work one round of ribbing 1X1.

Next round: *k2tog, p2tog; rep from * around; 91 sts.

Decrease 1 st; 90 sts. Work ribbing 1X1 for 4 more rounds.

Bind off all stitches in pattern.

Lisbon's famous mosaic sidewalks not only add to the beauty of the city but also are a source of inspiration for designers.

Cascais Woman's Vest
Cascais Colete Feminino

Specifications

Size: women's small (medium, large, extra large)

Finished Measurements:
Bust: 31 (35, 39, 43)"/78.5 (89, 99, 109) cm
Length: 20.5 (21, 21.5, 22)"/52 (53.5, 54.5, 56) cm

Materials: 7 (7, 8, 9) skeins of Cashmere Merino Silk Aran by Sublime (75% extra fine merino, 20% silk, 5% cashmere – 50 g/94 yards [86 m] each).

Gauge: 26 sts and 29 rows = 4" (10 cm) in Eyelet Mock Cable Rib Pattern;
20 sts and 28 rows = 4" (10 cm) in stockinette

Needles: size US 6 (4 mm) straight or circular, size US 7 (4.5 mm) straight or circular, or size to obtain gauge

Notions: stitch holders and 9 buttons

Experience Level: intermediate

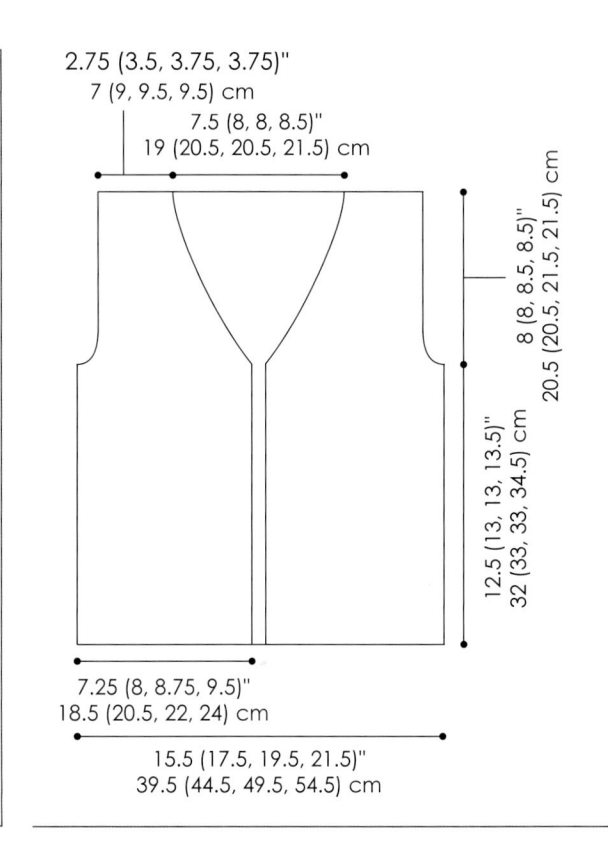

Eyelet Mock Cable Rib Pattern

Multiple of 5 + 2 sts.

Row 1 (RS): p2, *sl 1, k2, psso, p2; rep from* to end.
Row 2: k2, *p1, yo, p1, k2; rep from* to end.
Row 3: p2, *k3, p2; rep from* to end.
Row 4: k2, *p3, k2; rep from * to end.
Repeat these 4 rows for pattern.

Chart legend:
- □ k on RS; p on WS
- ● p on RS; k on WS
- ○ yo
- ╱ sl 1, k2, psso

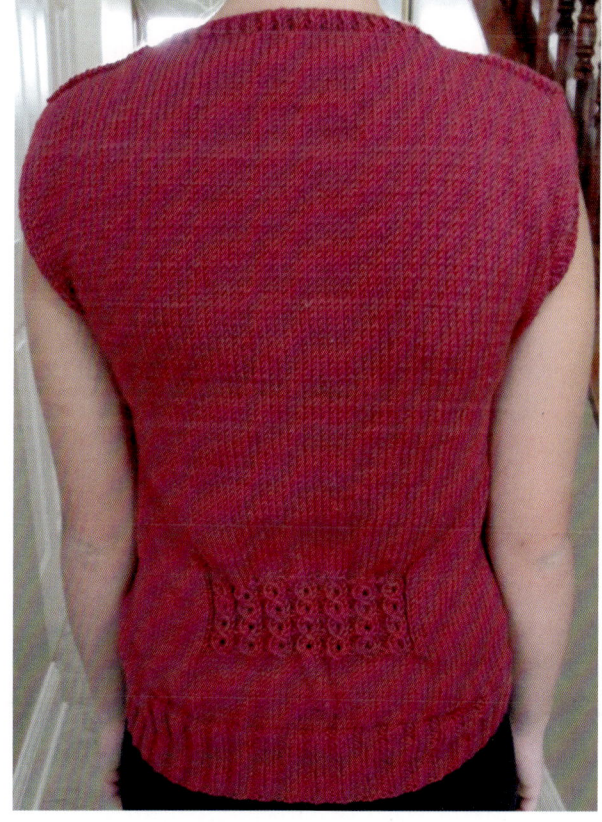

Back

Using larger straight or circular needle and Portuguese cast on, cast on 92 (104, 114, 126) sts. Work ribbing 2X2 (k2, p2) for 2.25"/5.5 cm, end with a WS row.

Next row: change to stockinette stitch and continue until piece measures 4.25 (4.5, 4.75, 5)"/11 (11.5, 12, 12.5) cm from cast on edge, end with a WS row.

Next row: k30 (33, 36, 39) sts, work the next 32 (37, 42, 47) sts in *Eyelet Mock Cable Rib Pattern*, knit remaining 30 (34, 36, 40) sts.

Next row: p30 (34, 36, 40) sts, work next 32 (37, 42, 47) sts in *Eyelet Mock Cable Rib Pattern*, purl remaining 30 (33, 36, 39) sts.

Work in this manner until you have 4 (4, 4, 5) complete repeats of the mock cable (16 [16, 16, 20] rows). Continue in stockinette stitch only until piece measures 12.5 (13, 13, 13.5)"/32 (33, 33, 34.5) cm from cast on edge.

Armhole

Bind off 6 (7, 8, 9) sts at the beginning of the next 2 rows, 3 sts at the beginning of the next 0 (0, 0, 2) rows, 2 sts at the beginning of the next 2 (4, 4, 6) rows, then 1 st at the beginning of next 4 (2, 6, 4) rows; 72 (80, 84, 86) sts.

Continue straight until armhole measures 8 (8, 8.5, 8.5)"/20.5 (20.5, 21.5, 21.5) cm, end with WS row. Place all sts on a stitch holder.

Right Front

Using larger straight or circular needle and Portuguese cast on, cast on 46 (52, 56, 62) sts. Work ribbing 2X2 (k2, p2) for 2.25"/5.5 cm, end with a WS row and increase 1 (0, 1, 0) st on last row; 47 (52, 57, 62) sts.

Change to *Eyelet Mock Cable Rib Pattern*. Repeat these 4 rows until piece measures 12.5 (13, 13, 13.5)"/32 (33, 33, 34.5) cm from cast on edge, end with a RS row.

Armhole

Bind off at the beg of WS rows 6 (7, 8, 10) sts once, 3 sts 0 (0, 1, 1) time, 2 sts 2 (3, 2, 3) times, then 1 st 1 (0, 1, 2) time(s). *At the same time*, decrease 1 st, 2 sts in from front edge, at the beg of every RS row for neck opening 19 (20, 20, 20) time; 17 (19, 21, 21) sts remain for shoulder. Continue working straight until armhole measures
8 (8, 8.5, 8.5)"/20.5 (20.5, 21.5, 21.5) cm.

Place all sts on a stitch holder.

Left Front

Work left front as for right front, reversing shaping.

Finishing

Join shoulders using 3-needle bind off.

Sew side seams.

Using smaller needle and with RS facing, pick up and k90 (90, 94, 94) sts around armhole. Join work in the round, mark beginning of round. Work ribbing 1X1 (k1, p1) for 4 rounds and bind off all sts in pattern on last round. Work rib around remaining armhole.

Using smaller needle and with RS facing, pick up and k118 (120, 122, 124) sts along right front, knit remaining 38 (42, 42, 44) sts of back neck, and pick up and k118 (120, 122, 124) sts along left front; 274 (282, 286, 292) sts. Work back and forth in ribbing 1X1 for 4 rows, and bind off all sts in pattern on last row.

Weave in all ends. Sew buttons to band on left front; place top button just below beginning of front shaping, then space remaining buttons about 1.5"/4 cm apart.

Museu Arqueológico do Carmo—partial view of ruins of Carmo Church, old Igreja do Convento de Nossa Senhora do Vencimento do Monte do Carmo, founded in 1389. This old Gothic church was severely damaged during the earthquake in 1755 followed by a huge fire. It was partially restored and rebuilt during the rein of D. Maria I. However, financial difficulties did not allow for finishing the project. The building still features structures of the 14th and 15th centuries.

Bibliography

A Brief History of Portugal, www.enterportugal.com.

Baber, M'Lou. *Double Knitting: Reversible Two-Color Designs*. Pittsville, WI: Schoolhouse Press, 2008.

Druchunas, Donna. *Ethnic Knitting Discovery: The Netherlands, Denmark, Norway and The Andes*. Fort Collins, CO: Nomad Press, 2007.

LeCount, Cynthia. *Andean Folk Knitting: Traditions and Techniques from Peru and Bolivia*. Saint Paul, MN: Dos Tejedoras Fiber Arts Publications, 1993.

Özbel, Kenan. *Knitted Stockings from Turkish Villages*. Turkiye Is Bankasi Cultural Publications: Ankara, Turkey, 1981.

Rutt, Richard. *A History of Hand Knitting*. Loveland, CO: Interweave Press, 1987.

Stanley, Montse. *Reader's Digest Knitter's Handbook: A Comprehensive Guide to the Principles and Techniques of Handknitting*. Pleasantville, NY: Reader's Digest, 1993.

Thomas, Mary. *Mary Thomas's Book of Knitting Patterns*. New York: Dover Publications, 1972.

Threads Magazine. Knitting Around the World. Newton, CT: Taunton Press, 1993.

Zilboorg, Anna. *Fancy Feet Traditional Knitting Patterns of Turkey*. Lark Books: Asheville, NC, 1994.

❈ Yarn and Needle Sources ❈

Andrea Wong
3625 Hickory Field Lane
Powell OH 43065-8175
Tel: (740) 881-3123
Website:
www.andreawongknits.com
Email:
admin@andreawongknits.com

Baby Ull
Dale of Norway Inc.
4750 Shelburne Road Suite 2
Shelburne, VT 05482
Tel: (802) 383-0132
Email: mail@daleofnorway.com

Cascade Cloud 9
Website: www.cascadeyarns.com

**Denise Interchangeable Knitting Needles*
1618 Miller School Rd.
Charlottesville, VA 22903
Email:
info.knitdenise.com/contact

**Lacis Museum of Lace and Textiles & Retail Store*
2982 Adeline St.
Berkeley, CA 94703
Website: www.lacis.com

Lovit Yarn
Fibre-Isle International Inc.
1280 Rte 177
Wellington
Prince Edward Island
C0B 2E0
Canada
Tel: (902) 888-4262
Website: www.bisonyarn.com

Qiviuk
Jacques Cartier Clothier
131 A Banff Avenue
PO Box 22
Banff, Alberta
T1L 1A2
Canada
Tel: (403) 762-5445
Email: jacquescartier@telus.net

StoneyHedgeFarm.com
2150 Marion Bucyrus Rd.
Marion, OH 43302
Tel: (419) 357-4184
Email:
judy@stoneyhedgefarm.com

Sublime Yarn
Knitting Fever
K. F. I.
PO Box 336
315 Bayview Avenue
Amityville, NY 11701
Tel: (516) 546-3600
Fax: (516) 546-6871

Sunday Best Yarn by Reynolds
JCA, Inc.
35 Scales Lane
Townsend, MA 01469
Tel: (978) 597-8794

Treliske Organic Woolens
2.R.D
Roxburgh
New Zealand
Email: Treliske@xtra.co.nz

Wool Cotton
Rowan Yarns
Westminster Fibers, Inc.
165 Ledge Street
Nashua, NH 03060
Tel: (800) 445-9276

*Knitting pin source
**Hooked-needle source

Index

A
abbreviations, 57

B
Baber, M'Lou, 48
Barcelos Rooster, legend of, 77
binding off
    as crochet, 50
    Portuguese method, 36

C
cables
    abbreviations, 57
    chart symbols, 57
    Cloud Mittens and Scarf, 54, 58-61
    Eyelet Mock Cable Rib Pattern, 86
    Manuela Scarf, 54, 66-68
    Portuguese method, 46-47
    2X2, 57, 59
    3X3, 57, 61, 68
Cascais Woman's Vest, 55, 86-88
casting on, 17
chart key, 57
circular hooked needles, 14
Cloud Mittens and Scarf, 54, 58-61
colors, changing, see two-color knitting
Costa, Tita, 53
crochet, binding off as, 50

D
decreases
    abbreviations, 57
    knit two together, 33
    purl two together, 33
    slip, slip, knit (ssk), 34-35
double knitting
    basic instructions, 48-49
    Sidewalk Mosaic Headband, 55, 84-85
Double Knitting: Reversible Two-Color Designs (Baber), 48

E
exchange stitch join, 57
Eyelet Mock Cable Rib Pattern, 86

F
Fancy Feet: Traditional Knitting Patterns of Turkey (Zilboorg), 13
Fisherman Sweater, 54, 69-75

G
garter stitch, 57

H
half-hitch loop increase, 31
headband, 55, 84-85
A History of Hand Knitting (Rutt), 14
hooked needles
    advantages of using, 50
    binding off as crochet, 50
    knitting from right to left needle, 51
    origins of, 14

I
increases
    abbreviations, 57
    half-hitch loop, 31
    knit in front and back methods, 28-30
    lifted increase to the left, 27
    lifted increase to the right, 26
    M1L, 57
    M1R, 57
    twisted bar, 32
    yarn over between two knit stitches, 24
    yarn over between two purl stitches, 25

J
Juliana's Baby Sweater, 54, 62-65

K
knit stitch
    Portuguese method, 20
    through the back loop, 21
knitting
    advantages of Portuguese knitting, 16
    historical perspective, 13-14
    resources, 91
    see also two-color knitting
knitting pins
    origins of, 14-15
    setting up and using, 15, 16
    working with two colors, 37
knit two together decrease, 33

L

lace patterns
    Manuela Scarf, 54, 66–68
    socks, 55, 82–83
Lacy Socks, 55, 82–83
lifted increases, 26–27
long-tail cast on, 17

M

make-one increases
    half-hitch loop, 31
    M1L and M1R, 57
    twisted bar, 32
Manuela Scarf, 54, 66–68
Mary Thomas's Knitting Book (Thomas), 14–15
mittens
    Cloud Mittens, 54, 58–61
    Rooster Mittens, 55, 76–79
motifs
    on folk sweaters, 75
    mosaic, 84–85
    nautical, 72–74
    rooster, 77–79

N

needles
    hooked, 14, 50–51
    sources, 91

P

Portugal
    history, 8–11
    map, 12
Portuguese bind off, 36
Portuguese cast on, 17
Portuguese knitting
    advantages of, 16
    historical perspective, 13–14
    hooked needles, 14, 50–51
    knitting pins, 14–15, 16
    setting up, 16
    see also specific stitches and techniques
purl stitch
    Portuguese method, 18
    through the back loop, 19

R

ribbing
    basic instructions, 22–23
    Eyelet Mock Cable Rib Pattern, 86
Rooster Mittens, 55, 76–79
Rustic Socks, 55, 80–81
Rutt, Richard, 14

S

scarves
    Cloud Scarf, 54, 61
    Manuela Scarf, 54, 66–68
short rows, Juliana's Baby Sweater, 54, 62–65
Sidewalk Mosaic Headband, 55, 84–85
slip, slip, knit (ssk) decrease, 34–35
socks
    Lacy Socks, 55, 82–83
    Rustic Socks, 55, 80–81
spinning and spindles, 52–53
Stanley, Montse, 13
straight hooked needles, 14
sweaters
    Juliana's Baby Sweater, 54, 62–65
    Traditional Fisherman Sweater, 54, 69–75
symbols, *see* motifs

T

Thomas, Mary, 13, 14
Traditional Fisherman Sweater, 54, 69–75
Traditional Socks
    Lacy Socks, 55, 82–83
    Rustic Socks, 55, 80–81
twisted bar increase, 32
two-color knitting
    background color, trapping, 40–41, 44–45
    double knitting, 48–49
    knit side facing, 38–41
    main color, trapping, 38–39, 42–43
    purl side facing, 42–45
    setting up, 37

V

vest, woman's, 55, 86–88

Y

yarn overs
    between two knit stitches, 24
    between two purl stitches, 25
yarn sources, 91

Z

Zilboorg, Anna, 13